SILVIO CANTO JR.
AND GABRIEL CANTO

D0792968

CUBANOS in WISCONSIN

ISBN: 0615714994
ISBN-13: 9780615714998

One October Afternoon in Wisconsin

I'd had my eye on the clock since lunchtime. I don't recall ever being so impatient about anything. My teacher would notice, I just knew it, so I tried to be as discreet as possible. When the bell rang I did not jump up from my desk like I wanted to, but walked quietly to the lockers ignoring my teacher's demand that we do our homework. She didn't like it when we dashed to the door.

We were walking quietly but quickly down the hallway when brown-eyed Susan said, "Aren't you walking home with me today?"

"Not today," I replied. I was probably blowing my chances with her, but there was too much at stake.

My brother, Joaquin, jumped in the conversation and with a straight face said, "You can't have him today. We are on our way to liberate Cuba. I will personally beat the crap out of Castro."

Susan looked at me and said, "Is your brother always the funny one in the family?"

"Yes. He got the humor and I got the looks. Bye, Susan." We took off.

Joaquin and I cleaned our lockers, said goodbye to the principal who was chatting with the gym teacher down the hall, and ran off towards home. The gym teacher yelled something, but I didn't hear him. We weren't in trouble the next day, so it must not have mattered.

We walked outside and met a group of boys by the bicycle rack. One of them, Johnson, said, "Susan is looking for Silvio! She wants to walk home with you! Did you hear that everybody? She likes you!" Then – with the best girly voice he could muster – he said, "You must be her little Latin lover boy!" sending all of the boys into hysterics.

Joaquin jumped in front me and met Johnson eye to eye. "Hey, Johnson, at least a girl wants to walk home with my brother. I heard that some fat cow is waiting for you around the flagpole. She wants you to take her to the ranch."

Johnson turned red, but the other boys kept laughing. I did too, even though the timing was terrible. We had somewhere to be. I grabbed my brother and told him we had no time for a fight today. We ran to the gate while he and Johnson stared at each other with their chests inflated.

On the count of three, we jumped the gate and landed hard on the grass. We used to do that for sheer fun, but today it was business. I got my pants a bit muddy on the landing from the wet dirt. Joaquin laughed and said, "You're in trouble. Your pants are muddy." Today I had no choice but to take it.

I learned walking home that my brother and Johnson had been feuding for days. I don't know what started it, but Joaquin was never shy about defending his family. In those days you didn't dare say a thing about our family around him, especially if it was about our little sister, Lidia.

It was usually a two-mile walk from school to our home, but we took a short cut through the woods. I was already muddy, so why not? On the other side we crossed a busy road, then jumped a fence. Hopefully no one saw us. We sprinted across a McDonalds parking lot and then climbed the stairs to our apartment. We speculated about the game on the way up. I told my brother that Tony-O would win the game in the bottom of the 9th—.

"With a walk off homer?!" he asked.

I snuck in so that Mom would not see the mud, but she saw it like always. I think she could smell mud. She told me to get in the bathroom and change my pants before sitting down for the game.

We were eager to watch the Minnesota Twins win the series, but Sandy Koufax would break our hearts that day. He shut down the Twins 2-0, and the LA Dodgers won the World Series.

We had a chance to catch the 9th inning on TV. Mom, Joaquin, my sister, Lidia, and I watched quietly as Koufax crushed the Twins. It wasn't close. Koufax reminded everyone that October afternoon why he was one of the best lefties in baseball history. Koufax was so smooth; his windup was flawless. He threw hard, but did not have Bob Gibson's intimidating presence on the mound. Gibson, the other great pitcher of the time, looked like a killer on the mound. Koufax killed you with manners and finesse. Not even Tony Oliva, or Tony-O, the young Cuban sensation, could touch him.

As we watched the final out, I felt stunned. I went to my room, stretched out on my bed, and stared at the ceiling. My little sister came by and tried to make me feel better. "Maybe they can play tomorrow. Maybe the Twins can win tomorrow," she said.

"No, they can't," I explained. "The season's over."

I wallowed on my pillow for a while, trying to recover from the Twins' defeat. Baseball was over until the spring and I was heartbroken. I grew up playing baseball year around. What was I going to do with my favorite glove? Or my bucket of baseballs? My mother noticed my trauma and offered a piece of flan, one of her best dishes, to cheer me up, but I said, "No, gracias." After a while though I had to laugh. I was a Cuban kid in Wisconsin crying about Tony-O and my team from Minnesota. I don't think I could have pointed it out on a map.

Around 5:00 p.m., I got tired of moping. I looked out the window and saw Joaquin out on the grass field across the street. I grabbed a football and went outside. We challenged two of our school friends to a quick sandlot game. I told Joaquin to "go deep" and we did our best imitation of Bart Starr and Max McGee. I threw the ball high in the air, and he caught it.

Just like that, we moved from baseball season to football season on that beautiful October afternoon in Wisconsin. Yes, we were finally "Cubanos in Wisconsin!" Our journey to the U.S. was now on track. We were throwing a football and continuing our assimilation into Wisconsin, a place madly in love with the Packers and football. It was hard to believe that we were in Cuba only 15 months earlier, but now we were playing a strange game in a distant land called Wisconsin.

This is the tale of the long and arduous journey my family embarked upon in 1964. It was full of unexpected twists and close calls, but ultimately we made it to our new home, Wisconsin, a place I had never heard of until a few months before our departure. For a long time my parents held out hope that my siblings and I would grow up as Cubans just like our ancestors, but Fidel Castro's dictatorship gave them an impossibly hard decision. Stay in the land of their parents without the freedom they held dear or leave that land with nothing and start anew far away. They chose freedom and a fresh start. A choice they made for my brother, Joaquin, my sister, Lidia, and me.

First and foremost, this book is dedicated to them, my parents, who gave up so much of themselves for our sake. Next, to my aunts and uncles who made it all possible.

I want to send a very warm greeting to my Dad's cousin, Ignacio, who spent 14 years in a Cuban political prison. To the thousands of political prisoners who endured torture and international indifference and the men who fought valiantly in Escambray in the late 1960s I'd like to say thanks. You were first-class heroes, each and every one of you. In due time, their stories of bravery and fighting against all odds will be related to young children in every language. I want to recognize everyone who stood up to the Castro communist dictatorship, whether on the island or outside, while I was too young to truly understand. These heroes taught us conviction. They displayed a courage that can serve as an example to anyone who holds their freedom dear.

Let me also say thanks to the American people. They opened their arms and accepted thousands of us. Every four years we hear Presidential candidates tell us again and again that America is an exceptional nation. I do wonder if those politicians truly understand what they mean by that. In my view, the U.S. is an exceptional nation because it was founded by simple men and women yearning to be free. They sought better opportunities for their children and faced huge hurdles. Yet, they met the challenge and laid the foundation for future generations. Americans took us in and embraced us as their own. I cannot express my appreciation.

1

I had never been anywhere so crowded. My mother, brother, sister and I were on a bus heading downtown for the first time to visit my Dad. It was miserable. My brother had to practically sit in my lap. Men were standing from end to end of the bus, grabbing on to the railings above and beside them to keep their feet. Every time the driver tapped the brakes, an old woman wearing a large hat and blue dress pressed Joaquin into me, which pressed me against Mom and her against someone else. I thought the front of the bus would burst.

"Silvio," Mom said, "do you know what it means to be a gentleman?" This was her way of telling me I wasn't being one. Two young ladies stepped onto the bus, and Mom was giving me a look. My brother and I stood up and offered our seats to the young women. They smiled at us, and I realized I enjoyed being a gentlemen. They were pretty. All the girls around were pretty. They wore lively dresses with giant hats and shoes that I could hear coming from down the street. I liked *La Habana*, I decided, just not the bus.

So far I had only lived in smaller towns, further inland on the island. I was born in *Sagua LaGrande*, but we moved to *Jatibonico* when I was really young. Dad had just been promoted, though, and transferred to the big city. He said he would now be managing a big branch in the retail district of the biggest city on the island. I wasn't sure what it all meant, but he was excited. He told me he was being rewarded.

Mom rose as the bus stopped. We had arrived. We walked a block and stood in front of Dad's new office. The window façade revealed suited men inside at their desks. Some were reading or speaking to clients sitting across from them. The door impressed me the most though. Every time someone walked close to it, the door magically opened on its own. I walked up to magic entry and sure enough it happened again. I stepped back and it closed, then forward again and it opened. Mom walked into the office, but Joaquin and I stayed by the door. We let it open again then walked outside then back inside.

"Stop acting like a bunch of *guajiros*[1]." I turned to find Dad glaring at us with his arms crossed.

"We are a bunch of *guajiros*," I said. He laughed at that, and turned back inside. Mom came out to retrieve us. She grabbed me by the wrist and pulled me back inside. For the first time I noticed a security guard in the corner, a short, stocky man in a gray uniform. He grinned and shook his head before walking over to the door. He must have been checking if we had burned out the motor.

"There's a zoo in town you know. Maybe I should let them have my two little monkeys. You'd be happy with your brothers there," Mom said. The security guard laughed. So did several of Dad's co-workers, but I didn't think it was funny. Dad introduced us to each of his co-workers, but they seemed to notice only Lidi. She turned red from the attention and hugged Dad's leg, but that only attracted more attention.

"You must be Silvito. I've heard all about you." I turned and saw a tall, smiling man with a suit as gray as his hair. He wore a nametag that identified him as Mariano Benet. He called me by the name Mom called me to differentiate me from my Dad who

---

1   Term meaning "country folk"

had the same name. "How do you like Havana? We have every-thing here. Food, music, baseball. Do you like baseball?"

I nodded. He chuckled and pulled a card out of his back pocket. It was Camilo Pascual, my favorite pitcher. I turned the card over to read his stats, then turned it back over. After studying every centimeter, I handed it back.

"Keep it," he said, "and this winter have your Dad take you to every game. They play right down the street you know."

I didn't know. I didn't know a lot about Havana. I had heard games on the radio but had never seen one, not even on television. I was introduced to everyone at the office. They greeted us with praise of my father and asked me when I would be coming to work with him. They needed another man with Dad's smarts.

After a half hour or so, Dad took us to a restaurant down the street that he claimed was one of the best in Havana. I was starting to figure out that calling something the best in Havana was calling it the best in Cuba. The more I saw of the city, the more I was reminded of images of American cities like New York and Chicago that I had seen on TV. When I told Dad that, he said the word I was looking for was *moderno*.

All through lunch Dad raved about his new job in this new city. He told us we would be very happy here. The schools were great and we had everything we would ever need. We used to drive to the big city to buy things we needed, now we were in the big city. Havana had been the economic heart of Cuba for centuries, since the days of the Spanish empire. Once long ago, he said, the Spanish called Cuba "the key to the new world." Now we were in the capital of that key. Not bad.

"Boys," he said towards Joaquin and me, "I've been working very hard for years for this. No, it was not a gift; it was earned. One day you will be men and you will know what it means to earn something."

Afterwards we passed by a shop filled with radios and TVs in the front window. Dad stopped and looked at a sign for something called an FM radio.

"I've heard of this FM channel. They say it's good for music," Dad said.

"Don't get any ideas. We don't need a new radio," Mom responded.

"Need, no. Want, yes. New job, new city, new house, new radio. It fits," he said as he winked at me. "It's been a good day. We can celebrate." He pointed to a wooden box about a foot wide. "That one." On each side of it were dials. In the middle, a hundred numbers that Dad said let you know what station you were on. It was an AM/FM radio by Philips, a very innovative company from Holland. Dad said many more details I didn't comprehend, but I was able to gather that it was fancier than anything we owned.

I couldn't remember Dad ever doing anything like that. He was always cautious and never bought something on a whim, but I also had never seen him so excited. We took the radio home and scanned the airways. The music came in loud and clear. It sounded like the band was right in our living room. Joaquin jumped into the middle of the room and marched his feet to the rhythm of a Cuban tune while the rest of us looked on and laughed. I liked *La Habana,* I thought again.

2

"1 4 ... 15 ... 16 ..."
   "No I saw it first!"
"No I did!"

"*Silencio,*" Mom said, interrupting the game Joaquin and I were playing. We were on the Santiago-Habana, a highway that connected Cuba from end to end. The sun was retreating in the distance. We were on the way to Ciego, Mom's hometown, where we spent a good portion of our summers. Mom's sister and grandparents still lived in Ciego in the home Mom was raised in. She looked forward to the trip home all year, not just to see her family but also because it was the place where she met Dad – a story they never got tired of telling.

As Dad put it, in the late 1940s his mother begged and begged him to go visit a family friend, an elderly woman named Luciana, who lived in Ciego. He was reluctant, but his mother insisted because Luciana had been there when Dad was born and helped my grandmother tremendously through a rough pregnancy. He finally did, and when he knocked on her door, Mom answered. Mom lived a few houses over and visited Luciana often. Dad took a look at Mom, and from then on he never needed any convincing to visit Luciana. He came back every weekend until they got married in August of 1951.

The cross-country drive was a marathon trip by Cuban standards – six hours – an eternity for an islander. To pass the time we counted the electric telephone poles that lined the two-lane highway, each trying to spot the posts in the dark first. I turned to Mom to see why she had cut off our game. Her eyes were glued to the stretch of road ahead of us. My eyes followed hers and I saw them. A soldier stood in the middle of the road, arms waving. On either side of him, a dozen other soldiers lined the edge of the highway. They stood orderless, some sitting, some standing.

"What are those soldiers doing?" I asked Mom.

"Playing *revolución*," she said. I thought it was a joke, but she didn't smile. Her face didn't move at all, and her eyes stayed glued straight ahead. Beside her, Dad did the same.

"Why are they …"

"Shh! Just be quiet. Don't look at them and stay away from the windows."

As we drove closer I saw that they weren't regular soldiers. They wore mismatched outfits and most had dark beards. A few men held rifles, but not all. I heard another passenger behind us grumble "*rebeldes*" and murmur something about the July 26th Movement. Other passengers looked on them with pride and celebrated what they were doing for the island. Cuba, as it had for much of the last decade, was ruled by General Batista, who had taken power by force years before and ruled with an iron fist. The July 26th Movement, which would in time become simply *La Revolución*, had evolved into a shadow war with the goal of removing the "president" from power.

The bus slowed as we approached, but didn't stop. The driver told us to be calm and turned onto a smaller road that the rebels were pointing to. He had seen them before. We had to take a detour, but eventually we were back on track. Some of the passengers continued to talk about the encounter and speculated that perhaps they had blown up a bridge further down the road. "*Distorsiones económicas*," economic distortions, they said, but those words meant nothing to me. Mom didn't want to speak about it. For a long time she didn't speak at all.

We made this trip every June. Leaving Havana was painful because of the traffic, but once we were beyond the city the road was tranquil. The countryside was green and flat, stretching as far as I could see. What I would later learn were tropical trees – they were just trees at the time – stood tall, at times clustered in groups of three or four. We drove by Sancti Spiritus, a very traditional town that I had heard was noble and religious. We talked about the city in school. It was old, very old, dating back to the Conquistadors.

We drove by countless *bohios*, or little farms, with straw roofs, tractors and cattle. At times we passed farmers, each leading a cart full of wheat or other crops, which were pulled by a horse or mule. Sitting in the back of one of these carts was a dark haired young woman. She must have been the farmer's daughter. For a second, I missed the country. I waved at her and she waved back. I turned to my brother grinning. "Don't flatter yourself, she was waving at me," he said.

Eventually we arrived at the station in Ciego, where "Mamama," my aunt Lidia, would always pick us up. We saw her at the station in a very elegant green dress, her blonde hair hanging halfway down her back, and her blue eyes glowing. She always wore nice dresses, always smiled, and never went unnoticed. She embraced my little sister, who shared her name, first, then Joaquin and me. Her hugs and kisses were an event: painful, exhausting, but full of love. We adored Mama-ma and she adored us. She would lather us with affection and cook for us all day. As soon as we got to her home she ran in ahead of us and grabbed whatever she had cooked for our arrival. After the long trip, it was always a welcome treat.

I walked in and saw my *Tio* Raul, and my cousins, Raul, Carlos and Maria de Los Angeles. *Tio* Raul stood at the door waiting to greet us with a cigarette in his hand. He always had a cigarette in his hand, and he always drank a beer for breakfast to go with a few slices of ham and cheese. Despite his affinity for beer and cigarettes, *Tio* Raul was very healthy and lived into his nineties. So much for bad habits. *Tio* Raul was much older than his wife, and was originally from Lebanon. He moved to Cuba as a child with his parents who owned a distribution business that catered to the local farmers. Yes, once upon a time immigrants went *to* Cuba.

Joaquin and I always spent a lot of time with the young Raul when we came to visit. Carlos was younger and very quiet. Maria was even younger, a sweet, adorable girl looking for a hug. Raul, however, was always up to no good and had a bit of a reputation around town for being a troublemaker. He was best known in my family for a picture that was taken on my parents' wedding day of him pouting because my Mom got married. I guess he wanted my Mom to himself.

The days in Ciego were an adventure for Raul, Carlos, Joaquin and me. Some days, led by cousin Raul, we gathered *lagartijas*, little chameleons that made their home in the garden, and released them into the house. We would hide and watch my *Abuela* Adelina scream at them and shove them out of the house with a broom. "*Tu no vives aquí,*" she'd scream, "*Salte de mi casa!*" Those tiny green monsters were a constant source of entertainment for us.

Once, when it was determined that one of them trespassed into Raul's room, he decided that it was only fair that the lizard face a trial. Joaquin served as the lizard's attorney and pled his case. But Raul, who served as the judge, jury and executioner of our courtroom, decided the defendant was guilty of all charges and sentenced our lizard to death by electrocution. The rest of us contested the unjust ruling, but Raul did as he pleased and carried out the sentence with a bug zapper. Okay, I'll admit that was very cruel, but we didn't have video games to keep us busy back then. Don't judge us too harshly.

A few mornings after we arrived, Raul roused Joaquin and me out of bed. "We're going out," he said with Carlos behind him. We knew better then to argue with Raul. He was the oldest by several years, so when Raul had an idea we went with it. He led us to the taxi station a few blocks from the house. A taxi station in a Cuban small town in the late 1950s and early 1960s wasn't what it is today in America. The taxis were horse carriages that were lined up one after another along the street. Behind the taxis was a phone that customers called to summon a carriage. We saw several drivers, or *cocheros*, strapping the horses to their carriages and waiting for the day's customers. Raul had his eyes on one of them. "Look at that one," he said, "the *gordito*." The man he pointed to was an easy target. Short, round and plump. His most noticeable feature was his dark, thick mustache that made his tiny eyes look like freckles.

Raul walked right up to one of the horses and yelled, "*Caballo, el cochero te va a morder tu culo*," and slapped the horse on the behind. "Horse, the driver is going to bite your …" well maybe I shouldn't translate the last word. Raul, as usual, found his own joke to be hysterical and turned to us in his triumph. The *cochero*, however, was not amused by Raul's warning to the horse. With his whip in hand, he started yelling, but we were already running. This wasn't the driver's first run-in with Raul, and he had clearly had enough. The driver chased us down the street, all the while yelling words that we kids had not been introduced to yet.

The driver was not made for running. His stubby legs could not match our youthful strides, and he faded quickly. His face turned bright red, and he struggled to keep his pants at his waist in his pursuit. We lost him in an alley and collapsed laughing. We just couldn't help ourselves. Joaquin stood up and put on his most serious face while he waddled in his best imitation of our clumsy chaser. We spent the rest of the day in much the same way, harassing the local residents. We walked all over town and left a path of destruction in our midst, all the while feeling like the Kings of the tiny town.

Of course, we were in for a shock when we came home. After the driver gave up chasing us, he went back to the station and made a few phone calls. What's great about a small town like Ciego is that everybody knows everybody. What's terrible about a town like Ciego is that everybody knows everybody. It didn't take him long to discover that we were Lidia's *hijos y sobrinos* from across the park, and he had called the house. We walked in and saw a very different Aunt than the one who had greeted us days before at the bus station. She wasn't smiling anymore and stood with her hands on her hips, never once taking her eyes off of us. She said only one word, "*sientense*," sit, and pointed to the couches in the living room. We obeyed and waited for the knock on the door that we knew was coming.

When I heard it, my heart stopped. The short, fat man with the dark mustache walked in, took off his hat, and turned to my aunt. Several times he apologized for taking her time, but she insisted that he tell the story. He told her quietly what Raul had said. He seemed incapable of saying the key word out loud in the presence of a lady. Now her face turned red, and she told him she would take care of it as she walked him to the door.

By the time the driver was gone, my grandfather, who also lived there, had joined the chanting. Their yells joined together into one incomprehensible sound that attacked from two sides.

"This is what you do for recreation?"

"You interfere with honest men making a living."

"You will all go apologize to this man."

"You kids need more work to fill up your free time."

"No going out tomorrow!"

I don't know who said what, but the point was made. At daybreak the next day, my aunt led us back to the taxi station and, one by one, we apologized to the man. He accepted our apology and seemed to be well past the incident. He chatted with my brother and me for a few minutes, asking us where we were from. When we told him Havana, he asked another hundred questions about Havana. He ignored Raul.

Our summers in Ciego followed that theme. We were boys being boys who fancied themselves the "Kings of Ciego," until we got in trouble. Then we would wake up the next day and repeat. We had fun, too much fun, and had everything we needed. We were never hungry and never bored. If the Kings were gone all day, no one worried.

On the day we left Ciego, I reflected on what a strange trip it had been while we waited for our taxi to pick us up. Soldiers on the road. Family scoldings. I couldn't decide if all of that was funny, but I laughed to myself anyway. My laughter turned to panic though when I looked up and saw the same cab driver who Raul

14

had tormented pull up to take us to the bus station. It seemed that my troubles from that day had not yet ended.

My parents had been out shopping the day the *cochero* came over, so they did not recognize him. To my surprise, the plump driver didn't bring up the incident. He even went on and on telling Mom what great kids we were. When he dropped us off at the bus station, he looked right at me and winked. A strange trip, indeed.

We took the bus back to Havana and made our way home. Summer came to end, eventually, bringing on fall, school and, most importantly, baseball. To be honest, I don't remember much of that year, 1958. I was young and it was mostly uneventful, but more exciting years would come – the wrong kind of excitement.

New Year's Eve provided a preview of the years ahead. The phone rang all through the night. In the morning of the first day of 1959, my parents looked like they had not slept at all. Mom told us during breakfast that President Batista was gone, ran off the island and hiding somewhere. We'd have a new president soon, and this time the people would choose.

At first few people celebrated, they didn't know if it was safe to. But less than a week later, a man on TV declared himself the winner and the parties began. Cubans took to the streets and gathered at huge rallies to cheer our tall, dark liberator proudly clad in his soldier's garb. After that I saw his bearded face smiling everywhere I went. It was on TV every night, on the cover of magazines and billboards. I didn't really understand. Not until the next summer when we went to Ciego again. I asked my Mom where the *rebeldes* were after the bus trip finished with no interruptions. They aren't *rebeldes* any more, she said, they won.

3

I jumped out of bed. It was Sunday and mid-October. That meant one thing: baseball. I looked forward to Sundays in late fall and winter ever since we moved to Havana. All Cubans like baseball, but in Havana, where the games were held, it was a way of life.

I dressed quickly in my best Sunday clothes because, to my mother, Sundays meant something else: church. I walked into the kitchen where she greeted me with our typical weekend breakfast, *pan con leche* and a very loaded omelet packed with beef, chorizo, onions and probably other ingredients I can't remember. *Pan con leche* just means bread with milk, and that's all it was. We would take our toast, dip it in the milk and enjoy. For several minutes the food remained untouched while I sat distracted by the baseball statistics in the newspaper. The season had started the previous week, but I had not had a chance to see a game yet. Since it was opening week, the newspaper was full of recaps of the previous year and predictions for the year to come. When I had eaten enough to justify leaving the table, I went into Joaquin's room and I passed the predictions off as my own. "Since you know everything," he said, "who's gonna win today?" He wasn't even out of bed yet.

"Cienfuegos of course. They have Pascual." I grew quite fond of Camilo Pascual after my father's co-worker gave me his card. He also played for the Washington Senators in the Major Leagues in the spring and summer and represented Cuba well.

The Cuban Winter League back then had four teams: *La Habana Leones, Almendares Alacranes* (scorpions), *Mariano Tigres* and *Cienfuegos Elefantes*. They were also known by their colors, red, blue, orange and green respectively. Dad grew up as a fan of *Almendares*, the blue team, and Mom was a fan of *La Habana*, the red team. They grew up in the interior of the island, so they never actually saw a game until we moved to Havana. Dad took us almost every Sunday, but Mom went only a couple times. *La Habana* and *Almendares* were the most popular teams of the league and played each other every Sunday afternoon after the other two teams. They were the Cuban version of the Yankees-Red Sox rivalry.

Each team played the others throughout the week, but every Sunday the league held the same double header in the same order. Joaquin and I rooted for *Cienfuegos*, the green team, mostly to rebel against our parents, but also to cheer for Pascual. He was my first baseball idol and had led *Cienfuegos* to the championship the year before.

Our bantering continued as Joaquin got dressed and ate his own breakfast. Finally, Mom reminded us all that we were going to Mass and baseball must wait. Our church was a very large, traditional building close by. We walked there as a family. Mom wore a bright red dress that ended at the top of her calf, tall heels and white gloves. She walked hand in hand with Lidia, who did her best to emulate Mom's fashions. Dad, like many men there, wore a *guayabera*, a light colored, buttoned up shirt that Cuban men wore to every occasion it seemed, and slacks. The church wasn't quite a cathedral, but it was big, old and full of statues. The front was made of tan bricks that rose into elaborate arches topped with crosses. It looked like a mini version of the famous cathedrals in Mexico City and many other Latin-American cities.

I don't recall what was said at church, I was too excited. When it ended I did my best to herd my family out of the building and back to the house. Mom had a tendency to find friend after friend to catch up with after Mass. When I finally got her attention, Joaquin reminded me of something very important.

"*El ticket!*"

It was a requirement that every student at my school, the Maristas Catholic School, get proof that they went to Mass. We ran to the church office and got in line behind many other children trying to get a ticket for themselves. The line moved much too slowly. Other kids' murmurs indicated that I was not the only restless boy trying to make it to a baseball game. When we got to the front, the priest grabbed two small pieces of paper, no bigger than a postcard, and stamped them. He then initialed the cards and reached out to hand one to me and another to my brother. Before I could grab it he pulled the cards back.

"What did you think of the sermon today?" he asked. I was beaten. He would surely learn that I wasn't paying attention and tell my mother. Then she would decide we didn't deserve to go to the game. He must have seen the fear in my eyes because he smiled and chuckled. "Enjoy the game," he said holding out the cards. When I grabbed mine he held the card firmly in his hand and didn't let me take it. "Next week pay attention or you don't get one." He let it go.

The lesson was learned, but forgotten just as quickly. We turned back towards the front doors of the church and found the rest of our family outside talking to another family. Three times I heard the women who Mom was talking to say how beautiful Lidia was. She turned bright red, smiled and hid behind Mom's dress. Dad saw our presence and brought the conversation to a close. He wouldn't have admitted it just then, but he wanted to go as much as I did. We walked home, this time I led the way and set a brisk pace. When we got there, I changed into my green *Cienfuegos* shirt, grabbed the newspaper, and led my brother and father to the bus stop. We caught the bus just in time.

"Cookie went one for three yesterday, if he goes two for three today, what will his batting average be?" I asked my brother later on the bus. I didn't give him a lot of time to answer. ".500! After that if he goes one for three tomorrow his batting average will be—"

".444," Dad interrupted, "but no one hits that high for a whole season. .300 is good, .400 is remarkable. Now let me ask you a question," he paused and stood a little straighter. "If a runner is on third, and the batter hits a deep fly ball that gets caught but scores the runner, what happens?"

"It's a fly out," I said, "the batter gets an RBI, but it hurts his batting average."

"Wrong," he said smiling. My brother laughed, jumped from his chair and pointed at me. Dad looked at him and said, "So you must know the answer." That quieted Joaquin. "It's called a sacrifice fly," he continued, "because the run scores, it doesn't count as an at bat. The batter's batting average stays the same. The batter did the right thing, so his batting average shouldn't get punished. Sometimes in baseball you have to put the team first, hit a sacrifice fly or a sacrifice bunt. Sometimes you have to run hard and dive for a ball, run into a wall. Catchers have to throw their bodies in front of wild pitches or block home plate. All these things hurt, but they must be done if you want to win. It's the same in life. We must do what is best for our family, our country or our friends even when it might not be what you would do for yourself. What you learn from baseball is also true in life."

For the next few minutes we rode in silence. Many baseball lessons had been passed to me during our pre-game bus rides, how to calculate ERA's or the importance of the cutoff man, but never had he taught me a lesson about life. I studied Dad for a moment. He had been quieter lately. Often time he and Mom would stop talking as soon as I walked into the room. Mom would keep a serious expression on her face, but Dad would turn to me, smile and ask about my day.

"*El Cerro*," Joaquin yelled, pointing to the approaching stadium. The sight of *El Cerro* brought me back to baseball and my idols. *El Cerro* was not as large as its counterparts in New York or Boston, but it was the most respectable stadium outside of the United States at that time. The playing surface was well kept, and it held about

25,000 fans, resembling today's college or Minor League ballparks all over America. The bleachers stretched from flagpole to foul pole around home plate. The outfield had no seats, just grassy areas where spectators could sit and watch. At very big games fans would even stand on the field along the foul lines and sit inside of the outfield wall. That would never happen at a Major League game. If a ball was hit near the fans on the field, they scattered and let the fielder get the ball. It didn't always work out smoothly, but it was fun to watch.

We exited the bus and made our way to our seats. We always sat in the same place, about ten rows back with first base right in front of us. When we sat down I took in the scene. I loved the smell of the freshly cut grass and the sounds of bats hitting balls during batting practice. We were early, but the stadium was already filling up. Merchants roamed the bleachers selling peanuts, drinks and Cuban sandwiches, the Cuban version of a game day hotdog. Near each dugout the teams' bands set up and tuned their instruments. The bands were salsa bands equipped with bongos, trumpets and other instruments I couldn't name. Every time a team scored or came up with a big out, that team's band would erupt into the team's anthem and the fans sang along. Throughout the game they often played short rhythms or melodies to keep the fans entertained. I was reminded of these bands many years later when I attended my sons' high school football games in Texas. There was always a band playing a song, a drum line hammering a beat or a chant in the crowd during the football games, and it was the same when I was a kid at these baseball games.

Everywhere I looked kids ran wild. Adults sat, smoked cigars and drank beer. We impatiently waited for the start of the first game of the double header. *Cienfuegos* and *Mariano* played first, followed by *Almendares* and *La Habana*. All four teams took batting practice before the first game, and you could often see two teams in the same dugout near the end of first game. Finally, *Cienfuegos* took the field to warm up, and Pascual took the mound to a roar of applause. I watched each delivery closely. He was so smooth, so effortless, but what was most spectacular to me was his curve ball.

For a long time I had been trying to emulate his curve ball, but I could never figure how he made the ball dance like that. It just didn't seem possible. I tried and tried, but it would be years before I figured it out.

When he was done warming up, the *Mariano* player stepped into the batter's box. Pascual's first pitch was a gem that flew right by the batter before he could blink. The next was fouled off further down the line to our right. The fan who caught it did something that an American observer today would think was very odd. He threw the ball back on to the field to a man we called *Bicicleta* or Bicycle. He was a short, heavyset man, but he earned his name because he could somehow move extremely fast. His job was to run to either side of the field to fetch balls that had made their way into the stands. These games didn't have the unlimited supply of balls that American games have today, so when a ball went out of play *Bicicleta* tracked it down, whether the fan wanted to give it back or not.

On the third pitch Pascual threw his famous curve and the batter missed it so badly that he nearly swung his way out of his shoes. The Cienfuegos band played a short tune and half the crowd rose to their feet and cheered. I was one of them. I jumped, grabbed Joaquin by the shoulders, shook him and said, "Did you see that curve!" Either I was a little too excited after just one out or he had yet to learn to appreciate the magic of a perfect curve ball because he just looked at me and shrugged me off of him. Pascual retired the next two batters and *Cienfuegos* was off the field.

Cienfuegos was unable to score in the bottom half of the inning, and the game settled into a slow pitchers' duel. Pascual was unhittable; he even took down the great Minnie Miñoso three times. After a few innings, Dad bought Joaquin and me sodas and peanuts. We ate and drank and made a huge mess. Behind us, a man yelled, "*Un peso que tira un strike.*" (A *peso* that he throws a strike.) I turned around and saw an old man with a blue *La Habana* hat and a gray beard standing and looking around for someone to take his offer. Finally a younger man to his right took the bet and lost. The young man tossed the older man a coin and then said, "*otra ves.*"

21

(Again.) This went on for half an inning until the young man had earned his money back and much more. I heard other fans talking about similar bets. A *peso* for a strike, five *pesos* he gets a hit, ten he strikes him out. Every wager found a taker, no matter how big or how small.

Late in the game, Pascual was taken out of the game that was still tied 0-0. The man with a blue hat from earlier immediately declared that the new pitcher, who I had never heard of, was going to allow a run and blow the game. He was willing to bet forty *pesos* on it, he claimed. The same young man from earlier took the bet and once again he won. Cienfuegos made it out of that inning without allowing a run, and the old man was furious. He screamed words that I had never heard before at the pitcher, at the umpire, at everyone it seemed. Dad stood up, turned to him and reminded him that there were kids around. His eyes grew wide and his face turned red. He apologized many times and even bought us each a soda.

In the bottom of the ninth, the game remained tied. *Cienfuegos* managed to get a runner to second with two outs left. It was up to Leo Cardenas, another Major Leaguer, at the plate to bring the runner home. The crowd rose to their feet as he stepped into the box. All around me I heard shouting, some aimed at the pitcher, some at the batter. The pitcher turned to second base to check on the runner then delivered the pitch. Leo got a hold of it and sent it into shallow left. The runner on second darted and turned third. The left fielder got to the ball quickly and heaved the ball towards home, but a second late. The runner slid through the plate ahead of the catcher's glove, then jumped to his feet and hugged one of his teammates. In the crowd, *Cienfuegos* fans hugged each other as well and sang along with the band as they played *Cienfuegos'* anthem. *Mariano* fans threw peanuts and screamed in protest. Grown men pranced around the stadium with long faces, some with tears. Whether these were gamblers or fans I had no idea, but both took losing very hard. I jumped up and down and slapped my brother's hand. I screamed for Leo and Pascual, the heroes of the day. I ran as close as I could to the dugout to try to get the players' attention or an autograph, but making my way through the crowd was slow and I was too late. When I got there, the players for *La Habana* had taken over the dugout and were preparing for their game.

Yes, the day was only half over. The break between games lasted about half an hour. The players warmed up, the fans ate. Very few fans left; and those who did leave were replaced by new fans. The second game between *La Habana* and *Almendares* was typically more crowded in the stands and much rowdier. Dad was more attentive during the second game because he had an allegiance to *Almendares*, but for me the second game was a chance to relax and just enjoy the game without worrying who won. I did enjoy seeing other Cuban Major Leaguers who I had read about in the newspapers or heard about on the radio like Mike Cuellar. The Major Leaguers really didn't need the money they made playing in Cuba, but played for the fans. I was proud to watch them.

By the end of the game it was late, and Dad didn't let us linger too long. At these games, very few fans left early like they do at American games, and several hung around to bask in victory or wallow in defeat. Baseball may have been the biggest festivity of the day, but it wasn't the only one. The singing, the betting, the drinking were all reasons why fans came out to the game, and they weren't always done when the game ended.

We took the bus back home, ate dinner and I went to bed looking forward to the next few months full of more baseball Sundays. I must have thought at the time that my life would always include the Cuban Winter League and double headers on Sundays. Dad took my brother and me every Sunday. Would I one day do the same with my children? I was too young to know what the men on TV meant when they spoke of *libertad*, freedom, and a new day for Cuba, but getting to see baseball every Sunday with my family sure felt like freedom.

I remember that word being thrown around a lot those days, *libertad*. It was a dream we were spoon fed by the bearded man who looked like my neighbors. A dream that brought Cubans to the streets with flags held high. Cubans like my parents who wanted to see their beautiful paradise of a country prosper, and with it their children. The dream was too pure to deny, too intoxicating to question.

The dream lingered for a time, before the romance faded to reveal the reality. The reality that *libertad* is a word that any bearded man can spit. A word with no power to console once the chains have been set.

4

The bus came by our house early to pick us. Our school days started early and ended late. Mom woke us up a little after five and fed us eggs and toast. Getting dressed was the long part. Every day we had to wear a nice blue dress shirt, khaki pants, and, worst of all, a shiny white tie. With Joaquin and me fighting over whose tie was whose and my own struggles to tie it, I was usually not ready until the moment the bus was outside.

It was a medium sized, green bus with the words "Maristas Catholic School" along the side in white letters. Joaquin and I stepped into the bus and were greeted by a host of classmates, most of them friends. The school was an all-boys school with students from kindergarten to 12th grade. The students generally segregated themselves by grade on the bus. I was in third grade with Joaquin a year behind, close enough to sit together and share many of the same friends. I found some familiar faces, Ramon and Mario, and sat with them about three quarters of the way down the bus.

The school was on the opposite side of town, and the bus had to make many more stops after our house, so the trip was a good half hour. The bus would later take us back home for lunch, then back to school, and finally back home again. We spent half the day on that bus it seemed, but we didn't mind. Bus time was our time to goof off, at least until we incited the wrath of the driver. Monday mornings were always full of talk of the previous day's games, which in turn led to a game of catch across the bus with a wadded up piece of paper, the precise type of thing that would infuriate the driver. While the bus was stopped, he stood and turned to the back of the bus where we sat and threatened to tell our parents if we threw another "ball." We calmed down and moved on to a subject that had been the cause of much debate of late, the existence of the center of the earth. We had all recently seen the movie, "Journey to the Center of the Earth" (the 1959 version with James Mason of course), based on Jules Verne's novel. Every day for weeks it seemed we argued about it.

"It exists," I claimed, "Verne wrote about submarines and those exist now. He's right about the center of the earth as well. You just wait until someone finds it." I was referring to another of Verne's novels, "Twenty Thousand Leagues Under the Sea," which was written before modern submarines actually existed.

"You're right, let's start digging at recess today," said Ramon in a way that gave no hint as to whether he was mocking me or actually on my side.

"Let's do it," said Mario, "we'll find giant lizards and mushrooms!" The way he said it left no doubt that he was mocking me.

The argument ran its course, and we quieted when the school building came into view. The campus was surrounded by an enormous wall, inside was a huge two-story campus and a baseball field.

"I'm hitting one out today. Over the wall and into the street," Mario said. He made claims like this often.

"Not even Baby Ruth could do that," I responded. Years later in America some friends would let me know that his name was actually Babe Ruth and that Baby Ruth was a candy bar, but for some reason he was Baby Ruth to us.

Our first task on Monday mornings was to turn in our tickets, our proof that we went to church on Sunday. As the name indicated, our school was run by the Marist Brotherhood, a Catholic order devoted to education. Although our curriculum covered more than the history and beliefs of Catholicism, nothing was more important than our maturation in our faith. The teachers were *Hermanos,* or Brothers, in the Order, deeply spiritual men with little patience for deviance.

We walked into Headmaster Father Anton's office and handed our tickets to his secretary, who checked our names off of a list. I hated walking into Father Anton's office. It was the site of a parent-teacher conference I had endured with my father a few weeks earlier, and I had not forgiven Father Anton for telling Dad that I had been acting up in class. Every Friday we took home a weekly report card. A few bad weeks in a row would land you in Father Anton's office with your parents, and I had fallen victim. At home neither parent had forgotten about the conference and what was said. It was only a few bad report cards, but I had yet to hear the end of it. I didn't see Father Anton, and I left the office as soon as I could.

Once the ticket was turned in, the normal school day routine began. All of the students gathered in an open area in front of the school that resembled a drill field. We had to line up by class, youngest in the front, oldest in the back. The *Hermanos* made sure we were lined up properly. Then one at the front would blow a whistle, signaling that it was time to walk to class. It wasn't quite as strict as a military school, but it was close. The youngest class started the procession, followed by each older class. While walking in line, talking to your neighbor could earn you a serious thrashing. So could getting out of line, slowing down the line or performing any other kind of disruption.

School always began with religion class, which meant the *Hermano* that taught the class expected us to be even more serious than normal. Sitting near Mario made this nearly impossible for me. Mario just loved to torture me with well-timed goofy glances. He would make his eyebrows dance, grin and bear his teeth like a wolf, or blow his face up like a blowfish. It may not sound like much, but for me it would have been no different than if the Three Stooges themselves were my classmates. He somehow found a way to perform these looks without ever getting caught, leaving me to face the brunt of the *Hermano's* wrath because I could never stop laughing. It was these outbursts that had earned me the parent-teacher conference with Father Anton in the first place, and I absolutely could not get another one.

This day was no different. Mario played his game, I laughed, the *Hermano* scolded me, but I made it through class without serious consequences. Next up was composition, where we were graded not just on our writing content, but on our presentation as well. We spent many hours studying calligraphy and perfecting our handwriting. I recall many times receiving bad grades because my work, although correct, was not neat enough for the *Hermano's* standards.

The days dragged along: arithmetic, reading, history. The best part of the day was *merienda,* a mid-morning break with a snack. Again we lined up and marched outside to what resembled a picnic area. Cubans spent a lot of their leisure time outdoors because air conditioning was a rare commodity on the island. We received our snack, a drink, *guayaba* paste and crackers, which cost all of three cents. *Guayaba,* or guava, is a sort of thick fruit jam. We spread it on the crackers and made mini sandwiches. *Merienda* was a chance to relax and socialize.

I couldn't relax today though. Father Anton was looking in my direction. He was speaking to an *Hermano* and slowly making his way towards my circle of friends. Finally, he ended his conversation and started walking directly at me. I froze. No, not again. He must have found out that I was laughing in class this morning. "Mario is a dead man," I thought. "The next time I see him I'm going to ...."

"Silvio could you walk with me for a few minutes?" Father Anton was a short, old man who never seemed to have his eyes opened all the way under his glasses. Every day he wore what looked to be the same white robe. He walked slow and talked slow. Reluctantly I stood and followed him away from the crowd. He cupped his hands together at his belly and seemed to be fumbling for the right words. A minute or two later, he spoke.

"You've been doing much better since our conference I hear." I relaxed a bit. Okay, I'm not in trouble, I thought, but what else could he want? "Could you ask your father to call me when he has some time, I would like to discuss something with him." He paused and studied me a moment with squinted eyes. "Don't worry, you're not in trouble. No more than the rest of us, that is." He gave me a faint smile and bowed his head slightly.

I rejoined my friends and was interrogated about the nature of my conversation with Father Anton. I had nothing to tell them, I had no idea what he was talking about. If I wasn't in trouble, what could he need to speak to my father about? And what did he mean by "no more than the rest of us"?

After a few more hours of classes, we got to go home, not for the day, but for lunch. We had from one to three o'clock free every day. In Cuba, as in many Latin-American countries, lunch is the big meal of the day (like evening supper is in America). We walked out in our lines, got back on the bus, and a half-hour later we were home. Mom never failed to have something remarkable waiting for us at home. Dad would come home from work as well, so we were all together and ate *pargo* fillets, a tropical fish, with brown rice and roasted vegetables, delicious as always. My parents asked Joaquin and me about our day so far and what we had learned. We replied with stock answers like we did every day. After lunch, I told Dad what Father Anton had said to me.

"Ah, yes," he said, "*Operación Pedro Pan.* Tell him I will call him this afternoon."

"What's that?"

"Nothing for you to concern yourself with, just go to school and study hard."

When the bus came back for us, I asked Joaquin if he knew what *Operación Pedro Pan* meant as soon as we had stepped out of the house. He had no clue. I asked Mario and Ramon on the bus, they didn't know either. An older boy on the bus overheard us, turned to me and said, "You don't know who *Pedro Pan* is? He's the boy that doesn't grow up." This left me even more confused. The subject concerned me greatly for another minute or two. Then our typical school bus activities took over and the subject eluded me.

The school day resumed and ran its course. Hours later we were back on the bus home. The last bus ride of the day began with a very important act of defiance. We loosened our ties, rolled up our sleeves, and untucked our shirts. The bus ride ended with a very important act of obedience. We tightened our ties, unrolled our sleeves, and tucked in our shirts. I had learned long ago not to let Mom see me that way. Once home, I got out of the uncomfortable clothes and did my homework. Mom made sure it was always the first thing we did. She would always look over my work when I finished, and was somehow always able to figure out if I had cut corners. Call it mother's intuition, I guess.

When I was done with my homework, I went outside and played a game of catch with Joaquin until it was time for my favorite TV show, "*El Llanero Solitario,*" or "The Lone Ranger." I loved watching the hero jump on his horse, Silver, and yell, "Hi-ho Silver!" I was an even bigger fan of his trusty, Indian sidekick named, "*Toro.*" His name was "Tonto" in the English-language version, but that word means "fool" in Spanish. So, they changed the name in the Spanish version. No one wants a sidekick named fool. Other nights I watched, "Rin Tin Tin," the story of a boy and his trusty German shepherd, who grew up in a fort in the American Wild West. I loved the dog and dreamed of having one. For many Cuban kids like me TV shows and movies about cowboys and the Wild West shaped our perception of America. This would later be put to the test; but, at the time, I loved imagining that the West was still wild and overrun by bandits, Indians and cowboys.

I couldn't watch my show that evening though. Well I could, but I kept getting distracted. I heard the sound of Mom's voice in the dining room. She was talking to Dad, and kept shouting the same thing over and over again. "This isn't our Cuba. This isn't our Cuba." When my irritation hit the breaking point, I rose and walked towards the door. I was going to tell them to keep it down because I couldn't hear the TV, but when I was nearly to the door I stopped. Something was wrong. Mom was yelling frantically and not giving Dad a chance to speak. "This isn't our Cuba. This isn't our Cuba." I pressed my body along the wall right by the doorway and listened.

"Please relax *Angela*," Dad pleaded.

"How can I relax? It's bad enough that you're speaking of sending away our children."

"It's just an option, but we should think about it. *Operación Pedro Pan* they call it, a chance to get them out before things get even worse." There it was again, *Pedro Pan*. A chance to send us away? Send us where? Why?

"No, I won't do it. They're my children, we go together or stay."

"There's more though. Father Anton suspects that the school will be closed soon. He says he is hearing that all priests will be banished from the island."

"So we will have to send our kids to their schools. It's not our choice anymore. What happened to *la revolución*? Casting out our priests. Fidel said he'd give us *libertad*. Does he even know what that means?"

Fidel? She was upset about Fidel Castro, the bearded man? That couldn't be, she cheered his name when Batista was run off the island. We watched him every night. He was brave, she said, and a great Cuban. Now she was scolding him.

"I know. This wasn't what we asked for or what we supported. Fidel spoke of democracy, but where is it? Even Ignacio is starting to turn." Dad's cousin, Ignacio, was a doctor whom my Dad grew up with in Sagua La Grande. He lived in Havana, as well, and visited us often ever since we moved there. Ignacio always came bearing gifts, and he sat and joked with us like an extra uncle. He told us Fidel would bring our generation opportunities Cuban children had never had and that we should be excited for the future. He spoke of Fidel as a hero.

"What did he say?"

"He's still concerned about Cienfuegos and Matos. He doesn't buy that a plane carrying Cienfuegos can disappear, and he was sickened by Matos' imprisonment."

I had heard those names, but I wasn't sure what they were talking about at the time. I could tell he didn't mean the baseball team. I learned later that Camilo Cienfuegos and Huber Matos were two of the original commanders of *la revolución*. The others were Che Guevera and, of course, Fidel and Raul Castro. Those men came to Cuba in 1956 with the intentions of overthrowing President Batista and eventually succeeded. In time Huber Matos grew disenchanted. Cuba's *revolución* had become Fidel's *revolución*, and he spoke out against it. Castro declared Matos an enemy and sent Cienfuegos to arrest him. Cienfuegos did so in a town called Camaguey, but decided that Castro was overreacting after speaking with Matos, his long time friend. Cienfuegos called Castro and told him that Matos was no enemy. After that Cienfuegos got on a plane headed to Havana and was never seen again. The plane was lost in a storm over the ocean, at least that's what we were told, and Matos wound up in prison.[2]

"We talked about Batista again." Dad said, "Did we get more than we bargained for when he left? He was a dictator though, how could this be worse? The tyranny was supposed to end with him. I pray he's overreacting," Dad continued, "but I just don't know. Do you remember what my Uncle Joaquin said when all this started?"

I did. *Tio* Joaquin[3] was the first person in my family I ever heard speak out against Castro. He used to talk about the crowds in the street in ways I was too young to understand, but I could tell that he was scared of them. *Tio* Joaquin was an attorney and a judge and had spent time as a professor at a law school. He was quite possibly the smartest and most well-read man on the island. He could recite the "Gettysburg Address" by heart, but he didn't just know the words. *Tio* Joaquin believed the words. He used to point to Castro's face on magazine covers, in newspapers and on TV. "There he is again," he would say, "the savior."

"He called it 'political immaturity.' Joaquin said people would figure out soon that it was too good to be true. I thought he was just a stubborn old man who was scared to believe. But, now Ignacio too. They are overreacting; they have to be."

"I pray you're right, or else what comes next?"

"I don't know. I just don't know."

---

2   For an in-depth look at these events, watch the documentary, "Nobody Listened." It's a gut-wrenching tale of what Huber Matos and other political prisoners endured in prison.

3   Uncle Joaquin was actually my great-uncle. My brother, Joaquin, was named after him, just as I was named after my father.

5

rior to 1961, there were murmurs – quiet dissenters who spoke behind closed doors. But, as the mandates increased, so did the backlash. Vocal Anti-Castro groups grew more frequent – new rebels against the old rebels. Friends and neighbors retreated to the Escambray Mountains of central Cuba to join factions who hoped to overthrow Castro in a guerilla war, turning his old tactics against him. The tensions grew with the New Year, and 1961 would prove to be one of the most consequential years in Cuban history. I was only eight, but I could sense the storm brewing.

In early spring, it really hit me that nothing would be as it was before when my father told me that there would be no more baseball, at least not as it was. I was devastated, but mostly just confused. What did baseball have to do with the men on TV? The 1960-1961 Cuban Winter League season would be the last time professional baseball was played on the island. After that, baseball, like much else, would be turned into a tool of the state. The professional players who left every year to play in America were exiled for the crime of using their hard earned skills to make money.

Soon my worries were well past baseball. My parents' despair was increasingly obvious. They were outraged with the turmoil around them sending the country toward a civil war. We heard rumors of bombs and fires in the city. Living in Havana, we were at the center of most of the violence. One day Dad showed up at our school in the mid-afternoon. The radio reported explosions at the Port of Havana and violence in the streets of the city. Where it ended, he could not be sure. He took us home where we were at least in his sights. From the front steps of school I could see rising pillars of smoke in the distance. Cuba was boiling on all sides. Castro's regime was growing more and more violent, as were the dissenters.

On April 13, 1961, a department store called *El Encanto*, which means roughly "The Enchanted One," was burned to the ground after explosions were set off inside it hours after it closed, killing at least one and injuring many others. The exact numbers, along with what took place during the criminal investigation, conflict, depending on whom you ask. The store was the largest department store in the city, and it was in many ways a symbol of the thriving Havana commercial culture of the 1950s. Tourists, many of them celebrities from around the world, were sure to visit *El Encanto* when they came to Havana to browse fashions from the world's top designers.

Prior to 1959, the store was privately owned and prospering. Castro's regime nationalized *El Encanto*. Like so many other businesses that year, men working on behalf of the Castro brothers came in one day and took by the threat of force what other Cubans had built. Employees who did not support *la revolución* found themselves out of their jobs. Many were outraged to see a symbol of what was their Cuba turned into another prop.

After the flames died, Fe de Valle was found dead in the ruble. She was on militia guard duty attempting to put out the flames. She was identified as a revolutionary, and her name became a rallying cry for Castro's supporters. Some people alleged that the C4 (a plastic explosive) used in the incident was supplied by the CIA. A man named Carlos Gonzalez Vidal was arrested after being identified as an employee of the store. He confessed to the crime and was sentenced to death by firing squad. Whether or not this story is the whole truth cannot be said for certain, but what's not in doubt is that the popularity of the store attracted attention from all sides. Many people took a hit the day *El Encanto* was nationalized, not all of them Cuban. By then violence had become the norm. The list of suspects was long.

Through much of 1960 and early 1961, tales circulated throughout Cuba that Cuban refugees were training in America for an invasion to overthrow the Castro regime. We lived with the assumption that an invasion would come eventually, but we had no idea where. Many Cubans believed it would take place in Havana, and this belief must have been shared by Castro's regime because the *Malecon*, an avenue near the port, was flooded with soldiers and heavy weaponry in anticipation.

One morning in early April, I awoke to the sound of a small plane flying overhead. I looked out the window and noticed that it was flying unusually low. The plane had to be involved in some way with the political tension on the island, but I didn't know on which side. Later that day I learned that the plane, and many others like it, was dropping leaflets, informing Cubans to prepare for the coming invasion. The hope was that once the invaders landed, citizens of Cuba would flock to their aid. We were ready, but unfortunately we were never given the chance.

On April 17, 1961 the invasion came, but not as we predicted. That morning Dad left to work as normal. He had an appointment by the Havana Zoo, way across town. During his visit he received a call from his office informing him of an invasion in progress at a place called *La Bahía de Cochinos*, The Bay of Pigs. Anyone loitering around the city was arrested and accused of being a spy for the invaders. Thousands of men and women were taken into custody on the streets of Havana. Rather than risk the trip across town, Dad stayed at his Uncle Joaquin's house on that side of town. I'm sure he heard more than one "I told you so," from the man who years before predicted the turmoil that came to pass.

Rumors spread around town that day. Some reported that Castro had fled like his predecessor years before. Others said the men of Brigade 2506, the invading force, were pinned down in the swamps, crippled by a lack of air support. Neighbors came over declaring that Kennedy had failed us, though my mother held out hope. Cubans watched the Nixon-Kennedy debates the year before. They heard Kennedy take a strong stance against Castro and hoped that his rhetoric would one day translate into direct support. That hope proved to be in vain.

Unknown to us, Cuban refugees (most from the Miami area) had been covertly trained by CIA agents in remote areas of Central America. These would-be liberators carried unmarked weapons and other munitions supplied by America; they also carried the belief that Kennedy would supply air support. About 2,680 Cubans formed Brigade 2506, but only about half of those actually made up the invading force. The soldiers who did end up on Cuban soil faced strong and immediate opposition by Pro-Castro militia in the area. As it became clear that the U.S. was unwilling to intervene with direct air support, Castro threw an overwhelming force at the invaders. The men were pinned down, outnumbered and outgunned, with no helicopters to get them back out to the ocean where their ships were waiting. They had no choice but to surrender or be slaughtered.

The next day, Castro was on TV declaring the invasion a failure. He called the previous day a victory against American imperialism and paraded the captured invaders on TV like trophies. The devastation we felt cannot be put into words. Castro had won; there was no denying it. Cuba would not be the place we wanted it to be.

It would be unfair to not mention that Kennedy faced an impossibly hard decision. The U.S.S.R. would have interpreted direct air support as an act of war against an ally. We all know the dominos that could have fallen from that. No Cubans deny that, but what we didn't, and still don't, understand is why he approved of the plan at all if he was not willing to give it a realistic chance of working. The men who landed in those swamps were put in a no-win situation. 114 soldiers in Brigade 2506 died during that very short-lived invasion. The 1,202 surviving soldiers of Brigade

2506 suffered well past the conclusion of the battle. Nine more died during transport to Havana. Five were executed for alleged crimes they committed in Cuba years before. The rest were humiliated, beaten and denied basic living necessities. Each was charged with treason and sentenced to 30 years in prison, although most were later traded for farm equipment and medical goods to the United States. In December 1962, President Kennedy and Mrs. Kennedy greeted these men in Miami. Most Cubans were less than impressed by the empty gesture.

Castro used the invasion as a pretext to justify a massive campaign of oppression on the island. Violence increased against anti-Castro groups or anyone who he accused of being an enemy of *la revolución*. Thousands of people were arrested throughout Cuba, many just pedestrians who were in the wrong place at the wrong time. Most were released within days, but some would remain behind bars for years or decades and suffer unspeakable injustices in prison.

One of these prisoners was Dad's cousin Ignacio, who disappeared in the aftermath of the invasion. Prior to the Bay of Pigs Invasion, he stated his opposition to the increasingly communistic Castro regime at a convention of Havana doctors. This public declaration would ultimately cost him 14 years of his life. After the invasion, policemen showed up at his door looking for him, but he was at his office. His mother, who was at home, called him to tell him to hide, but it was too late.

We learned in time that Ignacio was taken to a political prison in *La Isla de Pinos*, the Isle of Pines, a small island south of the mainland. By April of 1961, the isle was already host to 6,000 political prisoners, and that number quickly increased after the Bay of Pigs. I didn't see Ignacio again for nearly 30 years. He moved to Miami after his release in 1975 and spoke very little of his experience. I've personally heard other prisoners speak very highly of Ignacio, who used his skills as a doctor to provide basic care to other prisoners who were denied it.

What was Ignacio's crime that cost him 14 years of his life and countless beatings? Telling the truth. When *la revolución* started, he worked to rid the country of Batista's dictatorship. Originally Castro declared that the nation would become a representative democracy.[4] When it became clear that was a lie, Ignacio, like thousands of others, withdrew his support. He is truly one of the unsung heroes of Cuba who stood up to a dictator and communism and suffered greatly for it.

When things calmed down days later, Dad returned home bringing news of the invasion and Ignacio's imprisonment. I had never heard of the Bay of Pigs. A neighbor supplied a map and pointed it out. The bay is on the southern side of the island, opposite of Havana, and slightly to the east. This was not where Castro or anyone else expected an invasion force to land, for good reason. The area is swampland, not an ideal place for a thousand or so people to move themselves and their equipment efficiently. The muck is teeming with alligators and mangroves. This muddy land was one of the many obstacles that the invaders were unable to overcome.

Not only did the failed invasion result in mass arrests, but it also emboldened Castro and strengthened his message in the eyes of his supporters. The Castro regime nationalized what few independent newspapers and radio stations remained and any other business he could use to his benefit. For his dissenters, it became clear that leaving Cuba was the only way to ensure that they would not fall victim to Castro's oppression. The following months and years was an era of mass exodus in Cuba. Friends and family left with increasing frequency. By the time we began the process of applying for passports, my Uncle Jose had already left and my Uncle Orlando was getting ready to leave as well.

---

4   "There is no communism or Marxism in our ideas. Our political philosophy is representative democracy and social justice in a well-planned economy."-Fidel Castro. These words are verbatim from an English statement made to Herbert Mathews, a New York Times reporter. You can see them for yourself on YouTube: "Fidel Castro: Communist? Me?!" He repeated the same notions in an interview with Ed Sullivan in 1958 while he was still fighting his shadow war in the Sierra Maestra Mountains.

6

From the moment we declared our intent to leave Cuba, we became targets. To many Cubans, we were traitors or *gusanos*. Literally, "worm," but the word evolved to refer to any Cubans who left or were trying to leave. My parents held out hope longer than most, but in time they accepted the inevitable. When my parents married, they saw a future for themselves and their eventual family in Cuba, but those dreams were outdated.

The first step was a trip downtown to fill out paperwork. I spent one morning in May of 1961 in the backseat of a car with my brother, sister and *Abuela* (grandmother). Then, I spent the afternoon sweating in a nearly motionless line inside the passport office. Only *Abuela* waited patiently. Mom hardly spoke. She only muttered words to herself. Soft, slow prayers at the end of the line. Fierce, scoldings in the middle. By the time we reached the front of the line, her eyes glistened from hidden tears. We each spoke our names to a clerk pecking at a typewriter. *Abuela* spoke last, revealing her real name, *Rudisenda Gertrudiz Enriqueta De Los Dolores Joesefina.* By *Enriqueta*, the clerk looked up from his machine and stared at her blankly. Even Mom laughed.

When we walked out, we were *gusanos*. We weren't alone, but every week more left until we found ourselves short of friends. We had other worries though. Dad's bank was expropriated months earlier, but he continued to work there as long as he could stomach it, sometimes working out special, illegal arrangements to protect his friends. He worked for the regime that he was fleeing from, but that provided opportunities.

One day, his friend, Luis, who owned a distribution company, walked into Dad's office devastated. His business was going to be nationalized any day now and he would lose everything. He was sure of it. His son expanded the family business into Miami months before, but he needed a way to transport his resources to Miami under the government's nose. Together they hatched out a plan.

Luis personally brought his daily deposits to Dad who hid the cash in obscure files. From time to time, Luis recovered his money and purchased as many designer watches as he could. He wrapped those watches around the little arms of his nieces and nephews as they left the country in the months before his own departure. He then sold those watches in Miami and recovered some of his wealth. *La Revolución* gutted every Cuban business owner, but Dad's scheme limited Luis' losses.

Eventually, my father had enough. He resigned from his position, but faced a new obstacle. Being unemployed in Castro's Cuba was not quite a crime, but it was punishable. Unemployed men were sent to work camps throughout Cuba, so that they could participate in *La Revolución*. If a policeman saw an adult male loitering on a workday, he better have a good excuse. Dad took a job at a small bakery that was owned by another former client. He didn't actually do anything there, and I don't even know if he got paid. The job was just something to tell government officials if they ever inquired. Castro's agents were not shy about delving into your personal life.

Around this time, the food distribution system on the island was reconfigured. Rather than buying your own food, each family was now given rations. Mom waited in long lines at markets for her share. Prior to Castro, we were never short of food. If Mom wanted to buy extra food to host a party, she could. Now she had to hope that what little she was given was enough. Again we found ways to bend the rules. Our friend Nestor, who lived across the street, would give us his families' weekly milk ration because he was able to obtain his own milk from a farm owned by his brother. An illegal act, for the milk was not theirs to give away. Undeterred, neighbors traded goods to match their preferences – our sliver of autonomy from the CDR.

Castro formed the *Comités de Defensa de la Revolución* (Committees for the Defense of the Revolution), or the CDR, after the Bay of Pigs to monitor his citizens. The CDR turned neighbors against each other because no one knew whom they could trust. Would Mr. Molina report us if we told him what we really thought about Castro? What if Arturo saw our extra milk rations? The tension splintered communities and turned families against each other.

Every neighborhood had its own CDR president and council. The method of choosing demonstrated Castro's cleverness. They knew they could not trust Cubans to rat out their own friends and neighbors, so they brought in strangers to do that job. On our street, the government imported someone from a small town in central Cuba to serve as our CDR leader. He was a very tall, grizzly man named Mr. Bello who hardly spoke or smiled – and never looked anyone in the eye. Mom loved to say that he felt intimidated by the more cosmopolitan lifestyle of Havana. Most of the neighborhood was scared of Bello, but not Mom. She spoke frankly with him every chance she got. So much so that she developed a bit of a reputation that would one day cost her.

On the day Mr. Bello took his post, he made his rounds to introduce himself to his new neighbors. The visit doubled as a warning that he wasn't far. I answered the door to his loud knocks. He stood in the doorway, crossing and uncrossing his arms. He wore a uniform that tried to appear military. He didn't ask to come in; he just did it. Inside he spoke to my father in the living room. He asked Dad several questions about his new bakery job and often repeated answers back.

"So you were a banker before, a good one I hear, and now you're a baker?"

Dad produced documentation to prove his fake employment, temporarily silencing the man. As he sat, his eyes explored every corner of our house. He was either impressed with the decorations or looking for things we shouldn't have, probably the latter. His eyes met our Phillips radio in the corner of the living room. He stood to walk towards it.

Bello picked it up and dropped his guard. "This is a Phillips right? FM? Can I hear it?" Dad didn't react immediately, ensuring he heard him correctly.

"Of course." Dad turned a dial and found a station playing a fast paced mamba tune.

"*Increíble,*" he hummed the tune as he listened. "I've never heard a radio so clear."

"I bought it several years ago." Dad gave the man a long stare. *Before you people ruined everything.* Bello didn't notice. He listened for another minute before turning it off.

"I had better get going, many more neighbors to meet." He walked out the door still humming the tune.

7

In some ways, life went on as normal. We spent the rest of the spring of '61 on a less-than-relaxing vacation. As Father Anton predicted, my school was shut down and all Catholic clergymen were banished from the island. The only schools left were public Revolutionary schools. These schools gave Castro direct access to the nation's youth. The teachers encouraged kids to unknowingly incriminate their parents. How much milk did your Mom bring home? What did your Dad say about Castro?

When our school closed, Mom tried her best to shield us from their schools. Mr. Bello came by to ask why we were not at the public school, but Mom told him she was homeschooling us. That wasn't a complete lie. She did teach us some Cuban history dating back to the Spanish Conquest, and each day we had to read for at least an hour from the Bible or other books we owned. She couldn't accept the idea that the outside world was demonizing her religion. Mom did what she could, but in some subjects, math in particular, her memory from her own school days was less than helpful.

Our home lessons didn't last nearly as long as our old school days, so we had quite a bit of free time. Joaquin and I spent the days playing catch in the yard and our evenings watching TV or listening to the "Voice of America," an American government radio station that we were able to pick up on our Phillips radio. That was the only media outlet we had access to that was not controlled by Castro, so it was the only media outlet we trusted.

Those next few months crawled by as we waited for events that we could not control. Eventually we would get a telegram informing us that our passports were ready and approved, but until then there was not much we could do. We would have accomplished nothing by making our opposition to Castro public. Ignacio's fate had taught us that. There were still anti-Castro groups in the mountains and the occasional protest in the street, but by now Castro's hold on the nation was secure.

That summer once again we went to Ciego, although the recent events of our country made it a much more somber vacation than the previous summers. We spent most of the vacation answering questions about what was happening in Havana. When the conversation shifted to Igancio, well there was nothing we could say. Raul, despite being a few years older, was still up to his old antics. He led the Kings of Ciego around town daily, but there were times when even he paused to wonder. They really closed your school? What are they doing to Ignacio? If the mood grew solemn, he leapt up with a new mission for the Kings. It was his duty. He would not let men across the island ruin our fun.

Summer came to an end and we returned to Havana. In the fall, after a long break from formal schooling, my brother and I started at the Revolutionary School. We had to. Bello was always suspicious of our homeschooling, and he finally came by one day and demanded it. The consequences would be severe for my parents if we did not comply. Lidia was allowed to stay at home though, until she was a few years older. Bello knew better than to try to take Mom's little girl; no punishment could have intimidated Mom into giving her up.

On most days, it didn't feel that different from our old school. We learned a lot of math and composition, and we still had homework. But we also learned to fear capitalism and religion, tools of the American imperialists who tried to hold Cuba back and use

Cuba for themselves. I knew enough about our Spanish history to know that Spain used the colony of Cuba to better itself two centuries prior. But what that had to do with America in the 20th century? We were just supposed to take their word for it.

They played tricks on us. Maybe they worked on some of the younger kids, but I was old enough to see through them. One day I saw a teacher speaking with a young boy who I recognized from our old school. There were a lot of former students of Catholic schools at our new school, and at times we got extra schooling. The teacher, a young, innocent looking woman, asked the boy if he wanted some ice cream. Of course he did, what boy wouldn't?

"Well ask God for it." The boy looked at her puzzled, but he did as he was told. Of course, God did not manifest a bowl of ice cream in the boy's hands. "Now ask Castro for it." Again the boy obliged, but this time the teacher – lo and behold! – revealed the bowl of ice cream she was hiding behind her back. I felt sick. I never doubted what my parents said about Castro – he took Ignacio – but when I saw that stunt, I decided for myself. Why would he have to resort to such tricks if he wasn't in the wrong?

● ● ●

On some days Joaquin and I were able to just be boys. We played sandlot baseball games with friends from our neighborhood near a major hotel on *El Malecon*, a famous ocean-side avenue in the modern Havana. We did not have a formal league, but various neighborhoods formed teams and challenged each other. As you can probably imagine, *machismo* was in full supply. Our team was called *Paseo*, which means path. I have no idea where that name came from, but the team consisted of Joaquin, Mario and Ramon (our old bus friends), me, and other kids from around the neighborhood ranging from 8-12 years old. I tried to pitch every day and Joaquin usually caught. Joaquin loved to talk trash and no position is better suited for that than catcher.

Our friend, Tony, would serve as the umpire and attempt to keep order. He was heavyset and not much of a player. I think he would volunteer to ump to avoid the embarrassment of having to play. Games often ended with scraps. Other times one player would steal the ball and go home in response to a call he did not agree with. Joaquin did this almost every time Tony called him out. The ball was a limited commodity, so a protest like Joaquin's could ruin an afternoon. Many times I followed Joaquin home and forced the ball from his grasp.

The games that we were able to finish were some of my best memories from Cuba. Our games had nothing to do with politics or war, although some of the older boys used to crack that, one day, Castro would show up and nationalize our "league." We were stars on that field, just like Camilo Pascual and Minnie Miñoso, who we hadn't seen in years. Not even a dictator could take that from us, although his presence would make its way into our games.

Sometime in 1962, we began to see a lot of military anti-aircraft guns near the beach. It was just a few soldiers patrolling at first, but the numbers increased. Then they brought out the heavy machinery. It was odd playing right field with a .50 caliber machine gun 50 yards behind you pointed at the sky. Chasing a deep fly ball could bring you closer to those weapons than you would ever want to be, but most of the soldiers were nice enough to toss the ball back if it went their way.

Early on it was fun to watch these *milicianos* (militiamen) manning their anti-aircraft guns by the ocean. I recall telling my brother that they did not look like much of a disciplined army. Frankly, they weren't. Most of them were part-time warriors who were doing their revolutionary duty after work. In Castro's Cuba, you didn't have a choice about doing your revolutionary duty. Who knows what these *milicianos* would have done if America ever brought a complete army to their shores? Turn and run? That's my guess.

My parents scoffed when I told them about the *milicianos.* After the Bay of Pigs fiasco, many Cubans suspected that President Kennedy would invade Cuba to make up for the weakness that the failed invasion had projected to the U.S.S.R., but my parents didn't buy it. They said that all of the invasion talk was Castro trying to distract Cubans from the food shortages and dissension on the island. They were past believing that President Kennedy, or anyone else, would march in and save the day.

46

8

Another school year finished meant another vacation. This one, however, would be slightly more memorable though. I almost started World War III.

One Saturday night, Ciego, like many Latin American towns, had its annual *carnaval*. The town's residents gathered from all over, the local restaurants offered free food, and the retail stores set up booths selling souvenirs and other handmade trinkets. My aunt's home was right across from the central park where the *carnaval* was held, so we were always in the middle of the festivities.[5] All day we watched through the front window as men set up the booths and floats. As dusk fell, the action picked up and we joined in. The larger businesses and some of the unions sponsored floats that were pulled around the park as we lined the streets and looked on. For us the highlight was the firemen who drove their huge fire truck around the park and threw candy at all of the kids.

When night came in full force, the real fun began. At first dancers costumed in traditional Cuban outfits followed around the floats. The men wore straw hats and *guayaberas*; the women wore colorful dresses, cut high to showcase thin legs and high heels. Many of them wore their hair swept up, but still managed to

---

5   By the way, I heard that my aunt's home is being turned into some kind of historical marker because of its colonial look and location.

dance with grace. Little by little the dancing procession grew until the floats retired and the party flooded into the park. Local bands played customary Cuban music: a fusion of the guitar melodies brought by our Spanish ancestors and the rhythmic drumming African slaves carried across the Atlantic centuries before.

The party gave the Kings of Ciego a rare opportunity. We could play with fire and not have to hide it. Every kid in town lit up the evening with two handfuls of sparklers. The Kings led the charge. We ran in winding circles, leapt from ledges, and spun with spread arms until we burnt out, sometimes before the sparkler.

Later, we saw a group of Russian soldiers, three young men and a gray-haired officer. These blond, pale men stood out even in the dark. Not only because of their appearances, but also because they were the only people not dancing.

What brought *Rusos* to a small town on a tiny island? The Union of Soviet Socialist Republics, the world's largest nation, allied itself to a tiny island across the world that shared its ideology. I can't help but wonder how much Soviet Premier Nikita Khrushchev cared for the Cuban people. Was he using us for our location near America? The alliance offered the Soviets a chance to tip the scales of power. While Ciego danced, Khrushchev and Castro plotted. We saw a lot of Russians in Havana, but usually not soldiers. They were easy to spot. Their light skin was often pink in the tropical sun, and they lacked Cubans' affinity for style. The women wore plain clothes every day, prompting Mom to wonder aloud whether they wore the same clothes every day.

When my aunt saw the confused wanderers, she invited them over for *café*. They knew that word. Reluctantly, they accepted her offer and followed us back to her house. The soldiers drank the coffee and returned my aunt's kindness with an accented, "*muchas gracias.*" After this they relaxed a bit and showed us pictures of their families in Russia. They smiled, even laughed, as they told us the names of their children, parents and siblings. The officer had two kids, Alexey and Mikhael, the same age as Joaquin and I were. When I said the kids' names, I sounded the way Americans would later sound when they tried to pronounce "Joaquin."

Like most boys, we were impressed with their uniforms, especially the officer's hat. The enlisted men wore their regular Soviet uniform, but the Officer garb's was eccentric. He wore tall black boots, almost to his knees, a green jacket covered with medals, a thin, shiny belt and a matching cap with a visor and some sort of logo in the front. After about a half an hour of friendly, but incomprehensible conversation, they invited us to go down to their base and say hello to the rest of their "amigos." We accepted the offer without hesitation. Visiting a military base, that sounded exactly like the kind of adventure fit for the Kings of Ciego.

We woke up early the next day and started the long journey without saying anything to the adults, just in case they objected to our visiting a military base. The four Kings went together, Raul, Carlos, Joaquin and me. We maneuvered our bicycles down country roads that we had never explored, seeing only farmers carrying baskets of bananas and pineapples. We waved at them, but they did not even notice us. The trip took much longer than we anticipated, well over an hour, but no one suggested that we abort.

Eventually, we came to an entrance. It was not a fancy entrance like we expected, just a chain link gate with a few guards posted. One of the soldiers recognized us, smiled and waved us in. The base was not very big and probably had fewer than a hundred soldiers stationed there. We walked around and gawked at the hardware. I saw trucks larger than any machine I had ever seen. They reminded me of the giant iguanas in the *Journey to the Center of the Earth*. The base had a few barracks, a recreation area with a punching bag that some men were beating, and a small office in the center. In between were stacks of covered supplies. Raul was older and more aware of world events. He kept saying, "What are these *Rusos* doing here with so much military stuff?" I didn't care.

I broke away from the rest and walked through rows of the monstrous trucks. The tires were larger than I was, and the handle was so far out of reach that I would need to climb up the tires to reach it, and I did just that. It was open. I pulled myself inside, closed the door and took hold of the steering wheel. Four Kings? I saw only one. The dash was full of meters and dials of every color. I flipped a blue switch. Nothing happened. I turned a dial, nothing.

Then, I pushed a red button and an alarm went off!

The sound was painful. The base came alive. Men were scurrying in every direction, shouting panicked noises. Within seconds, although it felt longer, one of the soldiers pulled me out of the truck and scolded me in Russian.

Minutes later, a tall man with a fancy uniform, an officer I imagine, entered the crowd of men around me. They all fell silent while he looked at me, then each of the men. He clearly had no idea who I was or what I was doing there, and he was not amused. He pointed to the man closest to me and shouted an order. The soldier escorted me out of the base where I was met a moment later by Joaquin and company.

I stood shaken, thankful they had not executed me. Joaquin looked right at me with his hands wide at his sides. I told them what happened. Raul was impressed. Carlos was scared. Joaquin was upset I ruined the fun. We heard laughter from inside the gate and turned to find two of the soldiers from the night before. They mimicked my expression when they found me. Even I laughed. The officer walked behind them though and gave them both an earful. By the time he was done yelling, we were out of sight.

When we were far enough away, we slowed to share a laugh. Raul imitated the Russian officer speaking the strange language. One of Raul's favorite activities was imitating adults. He got off his bike, flared out his chest and put on his most serious face, then made noises that I suppose sounded something like Russian while waddling like a penguin. I nearly fell of my bicycle. They kept telling me that I almost started a war. At the time we could joke about it, World War III and nuclear war. Even the Russian soldiers could. The following October, however, we weren't laughing.

At the end of summer we went back to Havana and retreated into what had become our new normal. Then the "Voice of America" broadcasted a speech by President Kennedy on October 22, 1962. The U.S.S.R., Kennedy claimed, had missiles in Cuba. I thought of the base in Ciego. Was that a missile site? I don't know for sure, but I bet the KGB has an entry about a dumb Cuban kid who set off an alarm one day. My father understood the implications of Kennedy's words better than I did. He said World War III was brewing between the world's two superpowers, and Cuba was poised to be the battleground.

I heard more than one Cuban declare that the world was ending. We would be the first to go in a global nuclear war. The U.S. would surely bomb the missile sites. Then the U.S.S.R. would retaliate. The two weeks of the crisis were the most hectic time I can ever remember. We spent them glued to the radio. Every time we left the house we saw battalions of soldiers awaiting a possible invasion. Along the beach, anti-aircraft weapons were positioned, ready to target American bombers. In public, no one laughed or even smiled as we lived in constant fear that Cuba would be wiped off the planet.

For the United States, the crisis ended two weeks later when the U.S.S.R. agreed to remove their missiles. But, for Cubans, the crisis only got worse. We didn't know the exact details of the arrangement between the U.S.S.R. and U.S., but it was clear that the United States agreed not to interfere with Cuba in exchange for the removal of the missiles. It was rumored that Kennedy himself made a promise to the U.S.S.R. not to try to invade Cuba again. I don't know if such a promise was actually made, but I do know that, after the Cuban Missile Crisis, the United States left us entirely alone, guaranteeing the demise of anti-Castro groups still in operation.

Without the fear of an American backlash, Castro was able to send overwhelming forces against his dissenters. This especially hurt the guerilla warriors in the Escambray Mountains, who fell to the superior hardware Castro was able to purchase from the Soviets. Castro assembled a respectable military complete with Soviet tanks, artillery and MiG's. His ground troops were now well trained and armed. Fighting a guerilla war against Castro was no longer possible. These dissenters were killed or surrendered like so many other freedom fighters before them. Many joined the thousands of political prisoners rotting in the Isle of Pines, largely forgotten by the rest of the world.

The end of the counter-revolutionary forces was only the fulfillment of the inevitable. We had our hope placed solely in our exodus of the island, but that too would face serious obstacles due to the Cuban Missile Crisis. All emigration from the island was brought to a halt. Flights to America completely ended. The only way to leave Cuba by plane was on a weekly flight to Mexico or a monthly flight to Spain. My Uncles who had already left were able to take a flight directly to Miami and begin their new lives. For us the journey would be much more complicated.

9

E arly in 1963, Dad made an announcement at lunch. He knew our future home: *Wisconsin*.

"Where?"

"*Wisconsin*, here I'll show you." He walked into another room then came back with a map of the world. He unrolled it across the table and circled his pointed index finger across the northern half of the United States. "Ah, here." He tapped on the map.

I bent over the table to study the location. I put my finger where his finger was, then traced the distance south across America then east into the Caribbean and stopped at Havana. The look I gave Dad must have been transparent.

"Don't worry, we won't be alone. *Tio* Orlando is there with your cousins. We'll be islanders a thousand miles from the sea," he said with a laugh.

Tio Orlando had left Cuba a year earlier, so he had a much easier time getting out. He flew straight to Miami and, through the help of a church, was relocated to Wisconsin. The organization had given him the help he needed to resettle so far from home and had agreed to do the same for us.

He described the process in a letter to Dad, who felt like it was our surest option. *Tio* Orlando compared his new home to

Camaguey in Cuba, Mom's home province, known for its cattle ranches that dated back to the Spanish. That would prove to be a stretch. Dad pointed to the great lakes as if these landmarks were known to me and recited the names of some of the nearby cities.

"Madison, Milwaukee, Chicago."

"Chicago!" I knew that one. Minnie Miñoso played for the Chicago White Sox in the 1950s. I had read his stats in the newspaper years before. Wisconsin felt a tiny bit less foreign. Dad read more of the letter. It mentioned Wisconsin was cold. *Tio* Orlando could have been more specific. Cold meant something very different to me after living on a tropical island all my life than what I would later encounter. It was for the best though; the truth would have surely kept us from coming.

Joaquin and I lingered long after Dad was finished reading the letter. We declared bold claims of what our future home would be like. Time would prove us completely wrong, but at least we had a place to be wrong about. The news brought as many questions as answers, but we had a new hope. Our departure felt more imminent.

In reality, it would still be a year before we were approved to leave. Joaquin and I continued to attend the Revolutionary schools. Other than the constant praising of Castro we heard, nothing about the school was too unusual for us. We made friends, played baseball, and chased the girls around.

The major political events of my childhood were behind us: Batista's midnight departure, the Bay of Pigs, the Cuban Missile Crisis. We hoped that our remaining time in Cuba would be less dramatic. That proved to be the case, except for a few weeks in November of 1963. On the 22nd of that month, Mom answered the phone and gasped. When she hung up, she yelled, "They killed Kennedy. They killed Kennedy." Who were "they"? I had no idea, and neither did she, but that didn't stop us from speculating like the rest of the world.

We turned the radio to the Voice of America. It was true. Kennedy was shot dead in Dallas, Texas. I had no idea where that was and could have never guessed that I would one day settle there, but that's a different story. We didn't have much affection for Kennedy anymore, but we certainly didn't wish death on him. We listened to the broadcast of the funeral on the radio. The announcer described the somber scene as "John-John" saluted his father's casket. It would be a few years before I saw a video or any images of that day though. I recall thinking about Castro's funeral. Would Cubans mourn for him as Americans mourned for Kennedy? Would it come from an assassination and what would follow? I'm still waiting for the answers to those questions.

What really concerned us though was who did it. Was it Castro? If it was, would that mean another invasion? Some of us thought that, regardless of whether Castro was behind the assassination or not, Lyndon Johnson would use the assassination as a pretext to invade. Once again we lived with the daily agony of an impending invasion.

Of course the invasion never happened. In time, the event proved to be anticlimactic for us. We stopped talking about it, and the days slowed down. I heard a saying once about war. Something like, war for soldiers is short periods of intense excitement sandwiched between long stretches of unbearable boredom. The same could be said of our last years in Cuba. Dad continued to pretend to work at the bakery. He wasn't as vocal about his disapproval of Castro anymore. Not that he disapproved any less, but he was doing his best to wait patiently for our passports. Mom, however, did not share his patience.

As far back as I can recall, Mom has always been opinionated. She did not hesitate to say publicly what she thought of Castro and his policies. She was a Cuban woman; she had style. She wanted to shop at department stores like she used to be able to. Now those stores were all nationalized and shadows of what they once were. She wanted to buy fresh fruit at the market and spoil us with her cooking. Instead she waited in food lines and took home what she was given.

One Saturday afternoon in February 1964, while we were still waiting for the approval of our passports, Mom took Lidia, Joaquin and me with her to the market to pick up our food rations. An old grocery store had been taken over and converted to the food distribution center. We waited in the line for our food, all the while listening to Mom fume over what had happened to her country. Nothing enraged her like that ration line. It symbolized everything that had gone wrong, false promises, propaganda, mismanagement. "I wonder if Castro has to wait in line for bread," I heard her say many times.

On the way home we chanced upon Mr. Bello. He was out making his rounds, checking for anything unusual or citizens neglecting their revolutionary work. Once again, he asked my Mom why Lidia was not in public school. Lidia was 8-years-old, old enough that she should have been in the Revolutionary schools like Joaquin and me, but Mom had managed to avoid the issue for some time.

Instead of attending the Revolutionary school, Lidia was tutored at home by a very pleasant woman who lived down the street. Every day she came by and taught her basic subjects, math, reading, as well as Catholicism, an illegal study. I had several years of Catholic School under my belt, and my parents wanted to make sure Lidia could receive at least a fraction of the education I received about our ancestral religion. Mom ignored Bello's question. She was not in the mood. We kept walking.

Bello harassing us was nothing new. He knew we were not ideal revolutionaries. "I'm taking several of the local boys out into the fields to cut sugarcane," he said to us, "I'm taking him." He pointed at me.

"What did you say?" Mom replied as she came to abrupt stop. Her words were sharp. I had heard her yell at Joaquin or me plenty, but never had I heard that voice. The words were not directed at me, but I felt them as much as I heard them. This was not going to end well. "What did you say?" She repeated. She grabbed my hand as she turned to walk towards the tall man. I resisted, but she yanked me forward. There was no slowing her down. "You're doing what with my son?" He took a few steps back as she approached. His eyes widened. He looked around as if someone was standing by to help him.

"I'm taking him out into the fields with me," he said much quieter. "He needs to... He needs to do his work to support the revolution too."

"If you take him, you have to take me," she said, "He's eleven. He's my child, not a puppet of your revolution."

"That's not—" That's not necessary? I think that's what he was trying to say, but he never got a chance. He was not going to get another chance to talk during this conversation.

"This revolution, which my husband and I supported at first, is now a farce. No rule of law. No respect for civil rights. No room for dissent or an open discussion of ideas. This is not what we supported. So there it is. You want to take him? Then take me too. He's my son." I think she planned that speech long before. She sat on those words for a long time. I held on to her hand terrified as she dragged me closer and closer to him. The man looked visibly defeated. Surely no one had ever said anything like that to his face before. What could he do, arrest my mother? He either did not have the heart for it, or he was scared of the backlash. When my five-foot-two-inch mother was face to face with this six-foot man, he balked. He wanted nothing more of my mother. He told us to go home and said we had not heard the last of him.

His retribution was public, and, like everything else in Cuba at this time, it drew its power from the mob that followed him. I've spent a lot of time wondering how large numbers of Cubans continued to support *la Revolución* long after Castro had shown his true colors. A lot of them were acting out of fear, of course. The fear that came from loved ones disappearing and finding out days later that they were locked up for alleged crimes against the state. Some were still caught up in the fanatical ideas and viewed Castro as some sort of messiah. Most were simply opportunists. Castro had won; and, leaving the island was not a viable option for everyone, so some just decided to be "good soldiers" and play along. If you can't beat them, join them. Dad had an opportunity to do that. As a banker, he could have been a high-ranking bureaucrat and received all the perks that came with that: a bigger house, a nicer car, increased rations. Thankfully he took another route and was able to earn all those things in his own way.

I don't look down on most of them, truly I don't. The propaganda and revolutionary schools had been active for a long time, and who knows how many people legitimately bought what they were being told. A lot of people, especially the lowest classes, did benefit from the food rations compared to what they had before. I can't say what led any particular person to support the regime, and so few of them were actually in a position to do anything about it. But outside my house on that Saturday evening I didn't see ambitious revolutionaries or enthusiastic communists. I saw a mob of cowards.

Bello brought a crowd of Castro supporters that evening right to our front yard. There he led a rally chastising my Mom for her resistance to *la Revolución*. He knew we had applied for passports to leave, so he gave up on us. We were the villains. "Look at those *gusanos* who fail to support a regime that throws people in jail for talking. They'd rather go to America and be capitalists, slaves to imperial powers." That's what I hear when the events of that evening play in my memory. I see a tall coward from central Cuba standing in front of shorter cowards from Havana, bashing a woman because she stood up to him.

I heard his words that day on the radio. A lot of people did. The rally was broadcast all over Havana as a warning. Be a good Cuban, a good revolutionary, or we'll embarrass you and broadcast it on the radio. Joaquin and I sat around the radio occasionally taking glances out the window. Mom blew the whole thing off. She was past acknowledging anything Bello said or did. Dad refused to listen. Instead he paced throughout the house never out of sight of the door. Soon the police would come and take us away, and we would never get to leave. He was sure of it.

The police never came, but that day took a toll nonetheless. I was still too young to really understand all the events that had taken place in my lifetime. But I was old enough to understand that what took place that day was wrong, plainly and simply wrong. It was wrong because it was an invasion of our private lives, wrong because it was my mother being targeted, but mostly wrong because it was tolerated, even sanctioned. No government should ever mock its own citizens. No government should ever view the children of their citizens as tools to their ends. My views of the United States were based on movies and TV shows, in other words they were based on Hollywood inventions. But, Dad told me that day that this could never happen in America. Maybe they don't really have Wild West cowboys, but the United States would never try to humiliate my mother. That was good enough for me.

10

By 1964, Cuba was rigorously divided. Castro's supporters kept up their crusade, and the rest of us waited quietly till our day to leave. One day an official government telegram would arrive at our door with news of our departure. We had all our papers in order, so we didn't expect to not be approved to leave. But until we held that approval letter in our hands we wouldn't know for sure. "Any day now," we told each other. "Later this week. No I meant next week, it has to come next week." Early on Mom would greet us after school by letting us know that *el telegrama* had not come that day. Soon she simply said it didn't come in. Eventually she just shook her heard as we came in. No need to ask what it meant.

Winter turned to spring, and still we waited. Without news of our approval, we could do very little to plan our departure. Our options for flying out were limited. We chose the Mexico City route over Madrid because it would be much easier on our relatives in America who were putting up the money.

It grew into a family joke, the morbid kind. Telegrams were usually sent by motorcycle, so the very sound of one was enough to excite us. At the sound of the engine, Mom would leap up and race to the window, usually to watch it drive by. "I guess someone else is getting their *telegrama* today," Joaquin would say. Dad and I would laugh for a few seconds then sigh. A few times I saw Mom hint at a smile.

Our neighborhood was not the closely knit community it once was. Years of looking over our shoulder had done away with that. Friends didn't come by as often as they once had. Bello's rally ensured that everyone around knew who we were and what our intentions were. Everyday errands brought Mom cold stares and murmurs of *gusano*. The weeks grew longer.

Finally, one April afternoon, a motorcycle came to our door with good tidings. The driver handed Dad a plain white envelope. He ripped it open and looked for one word, *aprobado*, approved. We now had the certainty that we could leave, but by no means would Castro and company make it easy on us. First, a man, another of Castro's errand boys, came by to take an inventory of our stuff. Excuse me, their stuff. He noted our refrigerator, TV, tables, knives, forks, everything in painstaking detail. When he noted my Dad's Phillips radio, I closed my eyes and saw the radio as it was in the window on the day that Dad bought it. He said he earned it, but the uniformed man at my house seemed to disagree. I sat in a chair that had been in our house as long as I could remember, probably since before I was born. On the armrest lay a blanket Mom knit as a child. How can someone come by and tell us it's not our stuff? Whose stuff is it? I asked Dad hours later after the man left. He grinned and said, "The people's."

For years and years, I would return to that night. I laid to rest in a bed that belonged to *the people* inside of a house my family didn't own, surrounded by my toys that weren't mine contemplating what it meant to own anything at all. It's a tempting idea, I'll admit. *No private property.* Tempting to students on college campuses arguing about how the world should be; tempting when it's spelled out so eloquently on paper. What a paradise this world could be if everyone owned everything, right. No hunger, no shortages, no disappointments. But nowhere in all that rhetoric did I ever hear what the abolition of private property actually means. It's a man coming over to take notes on all the objects you possess but don't own, use but don't own, bought but don't own. Then that same man looks at you before he leaves and says, "Oh, by the way, you better not sell anything or give it away because if you do ... well, just don't."

It would be July before we were on a plane. There were a lot of arrangements to make. First, we had to secure a flight to Mexico City. Then, because Mexico would not grant us visas to enter the United States, we would have to fly to Jamaica. And finally from there we could depart to Miami. These flights would not be back to back to back by a long shot. In between the flights we had to find places to live and ways to feed ourselves. We left without knowing exactly what was going to happen, but the priority was to leave. We'd figure the rest out once we were in a free country.

There were no going-away parties for us those last few months. Most close friends and family members were gone, and let's just say we had grown apart from many old friends who remained and were committed to remaining. To our fellow *gusanos*, our departure brought hope that they could soon do the same. We saved our celebrations for when we met on the other side of tyranny. Some we did see months or years later, others we never saw again.

Only very young kids were sad to see their friends leave. I remember my little sister and her friend Maria from down the street crying the last time they embraced. Maria's father was very involved in the Neighborhood CDR, but neither she nor Lidia seemed to care about our families' political disagreements. Thank God for that because Maria could have gotten us in major trouble.

Days after the man came over to take inventory, we started to find cracks in the system. We lived in a duplex, sharing the property with several other families. A lady named, Hortencia, managed the property. We knew her well. She came by often, but always to examine a leaky sink or broken water heater. She then sent a son to do the work later that day. Hortencia came over a few days after the inventory and asked to talk. Befuddled, Dad accepted and let her in. She asked him question after question of the inventory process. Maybe she was planning on going through it herself or was just very curious.

Hortencia looked at our refrigerator. She had the exact same model, just years older and in much worse shape. She suggested switching them, probably joking at first. Dad mentioned all the things that would entail. We couldn't just carry it out the front door and down to her apartment; far too many eyes would see that. Slightly discouraged, Hortencia paced in front of the refrigerator. Finally she looked at me, smiled and said, "I'm a handywoman, I'll think of something," and left.

A few nights later she showed up with ropes and her whole family (Hortencia, her husband and three sons). They concocted a plan to lower the fridge from a balcony on the side of the house using a complicated pulley system. It was dark and the balcony was mostly out of sight. If they did it quickly and quietly, it could work. Dad agreed, although I'm not sure why. We didn't gain anything from the switch and it was a very unnecessary risk, but I think Dad slept a little easier knowing he had not left with his tail between his legs. This way he knew some of our stuff would end up with good people. The plan went off without a hitch. Joaquin and I watched both frightened and excited. After all of the underground activity going on around Cuba, secret plots and invasions, it seemed fitting to be breaking rules in the dark.

Not a soul noticed our switcheroo except sweet little Maria. The last time she came over to say goodbye to Lidia, she asked when we got a new fridge. Luckily for us Lidia was sharp enough to deny it and distract her. Lidia pulled her into a different room, and Maria probably never thought about it again. Had she mentioned anything to her father about our new fridge, it could have seriously delayed our departure or worse.

Looking back, there was probably a lot more underground plotting than I realized. I'm sure Dad was able to trade or sell plenty of our things, and I just never noticed. He is a very sharp guy with deep connections. Empowered by his success from the refrigerator switch Dad tried to do the same thing with his radio. He was proud of that radio. It signified a better time and a better way of doing things. He could bear to lose most of his belongings, but Castro would not have that radio. The inventory noted the radio and the brand, but not the model. If he could find another Phillips radio, much older and less valuable, he could trade it for a few bucks. In no time, he found such a radio and came home with cash in hand. The money helped to make our last weeks a little easier.

The plan backfired. Bello couldn't let us leave without saying goodbye. On our last day in our house, he came over with another man to assist in the final inventory check. Everything in our house was checked again to make sure it matched the list from a few weeks before. Bello had been in our home before so he didn't need the list. He asked about a chair he remembered in the dining room and a coffee table he must have made up. But neither were on the list, so all we had to say was we gave it away years before.

Bello paced firmly through every room in the house. With every step his eyes scanned another corner. In our kitchen he passed our refrigerator twice and ignored it. Disappointed, he stepped into the living room and sat next to the other government worker on a couch as Dad signed several forms. I sat in the kitchen studying his every move. After a few minutes of looking bored, he stood and walked into a corner. His back was turned to me, but I could hear his voice.

"Ah, your Phillips that you bought *years* ago." Dad put down his pen. "No this isn't right," Bello continued, "this is only AM. You liar! You thief! Where is the list?" He grabbed a piece of paper and ran his finger down it until he found what he was looking for. "Clever. Very clever. You thought you could make fools of us."

"I can fix this," Dad quickly responded. "Fifteen minutes."

"Fifteen minutes. Be my guest then, you have fifteen minutes to produce an AM/FM Phillips radio or you will be missing your flight to America." He cheered up like he had just won a raffle.

I stormed into my room. This was the end; we were ruined. Tears fell from my eyes as I lay in a bed that now felt permanent. Somewhere Wisconsin waited with its cowboys, but I would be here forever under the gaze of Bello and his hero, Fidel Castro.

But not even ten minutes passed before I heard the door open and Dad's voice. "Here it is, see no problems."

"How did you? No! You're a thief," Bello responded. His voice was higher now. He sighed like Lidia when she didn't get her way. The other man looked to be in a hurry to get out of there. He lacked Bello's enthusiasm for revolutionary work. He handed Dad the rest of the forms and told Bello there was nothing they could do. It matched the list. Bello sat in the same chair as before with his arms crossed and a long face.

When the papers were signed Bello and the other man walked us out. We stood outside as he put a seal on our door. I had seen those seals before. They indicated that a house was vacant and would soon be assigned to a new family. When they were done, Bello walked down the street without saying goodbye. The other man quickly jumped into a waiting car. We stood for a few minutes outside our home that we were not allowed to enter before a cab arrived. As we loaded our bags, I saw Bello give us one last look.

The driver asked Dad where we were going. Dad named the hotel where we would spend our last night in Cuba. Driving off I looked back and saw our house that I had known for so long. I saw Joaquin and me playing ball in the yard. I pictured the whole family coming home for lunch like we did before life got so complicated. Lastly, I saw the seal.

We drove by a little cafe where I had my first hamburger. I saw the sandlot where I spent a good part of my summers with friends; I would probably never see it again. I saw an abandoned building that used to be a famous restaurant called *Los Violines*. The owners had packed up and taken it to Miami a long time before. Now here we were doing the same thing, but with nothing. Our stuff had stayed behind, our money turned over. We drove on an avenue near the ocean and I looked out into the blue. Somewhere there was a different land where we would start over with a new house and new stuff. And this time no one would tell us it was not ours.

We were dependent on family members for the hotel where we spent out last night because our money was taken with our possessions. *Tio* Jaquin, who had predicted darker days so many years before, arranged the room. The night was a quiet one. I asked Dad where he got the radio, but he didn't want to talk about it just then.

I actually wouldn't learn for a long time. Mom told us to go to bed early to prepare for the long day ahead of us. She told us to pray for the coming journey. She looked spent. Her eyes were red and hollow and her face was pale. I never saw her cry, but I think she had when we weren't looking. She kissed us goodnight and paused for a long moment to look out the window before she went to bed herself.

Joaquin and I didn't sleep much that night. Our eyes were glued to the same window. It looked over the lights of the city, but they did not seem to burn as bright as they once had. All of the tropical island's beauty was cloaked by the night.

"Do you remember that time in Ciego when we torched the lizard?" Joaquin asked.

"Yes."

"And when Raul told the *cochero* that the horse was going to bite his –."

"Yes." My eyes were still glued to the window, and he must have noticed that his questions were not getting my full attention. He didn't say anything for a few minutes until he just couldn't help himself.

"Do you remember *bicicleta*? He was so fast." He laughed before he was finished speaking and I did too. "In America we can go to baseball games, right?"

"Yeah, we can go to Major League games."

"Cool, I can't wait." I couldn't either, but I had no idea when that would be. We would be in Wisconsin eventually, but what would come before that I could not say. Joaquin finally grew quiet for a while and lay down. In the silence, I saw pieces of my life. I saw the times Joaquin had mentioned and so many more. I wasn't dying, but my short life was flashing before my eyes. It was fitting though; my life in Cuba was dying. I thought a lot of Ciego and my cousins. I felt something I had never felt before or since. It was fear, nervousness, sadness, every feeling I had ever felt rolled up into one, far too much for a 12-year-old to know what to do with. As I was finally drifting off, Joaquin's head popped up one last time. "Do you think we will ever see this place again?"

"Maybe we will, but it will never be the same," I said as sleep took me.

11

The next morning was a quiet one. We each ate a piece of toast for breakfast then I helped Dad pack our few bags into our taxi. Mom sat at the kitchen table of our hotel staring straight ahead. She didn't eat her food or even blink. Lidia walked up to her and gave her hanging arm a hug. Mom pulled her close, but her eyes stayed still.

Tío Joaquin was so concerned that we might miss our flight that he hired a backup taxi to follow us in case the first was late or had a flat tire. It seemed a little ridiculous to me at the time, but he wasn't willing to take the risk. We didn't have a home or most of our belongings. Missing our flight was not an option. Whatever money Dad had stored in bank accounts had been taken from us along with everything else. We carried the clothes on our backs and a few changes of undergarments in our luggage that we were so graciously allowed to take with us. The rest of our belongings were back in our sealed house, or so I thought.

The previous night, while we were asleep in our hotel, the same neighbors who we had swapped refrigerators with managed to get into our house and take a lot of our stuff. Years later in New York City, where we met them one afternoon, we exchanged our Cuba exodus stories, but theirs had a twist. The day we left, they discovered that the seal on our door was not very effective. They snuck into the house that night and took our radio and other small trinkets that they could put to use. When they left they resealed the door. I'm sure whenever the next family moved in and saw what was missing they blamed it on us. Oh well, any small victory we could win against Castro was worth it. We were so excited to hear our neighbors' story. Once again, we knew our belongings had ended up with good people.

I would also learn in time how my Dad had managed to magically produce the correct radio the day before. He walked to another neighbor who he knew owned the same radio and told him we were in trouble. He didn't have any money left to buy the radio, but the neighbor gave it to him and told him to pay him back when they saw each other in America.

These were not insignificant acts of defiance. They represent why men like Castro will always fail. They cannot watch everyone at all times. Cubans stuck together. Whether it was the black market milk trade, exploiting Castro's property policies, or making arrangements for hotels and taxis for family members who already had everything they owned taken away, Cubans found whatever freedom slipped through the cracks. There were men who took up arms against Castro, many men, but they weren't the only ones fighting. Every time a Cuban broke a rule he believed to be unjust or expressed a suppressed truth, he was fighting against tyranny. This fight continues to this day.

As we drove to the airport, we passed the Maristas Catholic School, our old school. I pointed it out to my brother, but he covered his eyes. The moment had clearly gotten to him. There would be no more "remember when." We didn't want to start talking like we were gone until we were actually gone. Plenty could still go wrong, especially at the airport. Each of our relatives warned my Dad about what happens at the airport. The inspection, as he called it, would not be fun, but he spared me the details.

The driver dropped us off at the gate of the Havana Airport. The backup taxi came to a stop behind the first taxi and the driver gave my father a long look before driving off. We found ourselves surrounded by other families who were in the same position as we were. We saw sunken eyes and pale faces on the adults, tears in the eyes of the young children. Inside we lined up for what we were dreading, the inspection. No one spoke while we waited except mothers soothing their confused children. Words attracted attention and no one wanted that. We were *gusanos* all. The men who were standing between the airplane and us held government positions. Some took their job more seriously than others. A few enjoyed it.

Blue-suited policemen separated everyone into two groups. To the left side of the room went the women, each surrounded by her children if she had any. To the right, the men. I watched my father as he was led to another room, then both male and female police officers led us into an adjacent room. We spread out across the empty room while a group of officers inspected each family individually. We stood towards the back of the room and watched the first family walk behind a tarp in the corner. A female inspector would verify that the woman was not taking anything out of the country, the children as well. There was only one way to be positive. The mother and her two children looked ill as they emerged from behind the tarp. A few families followed.

Suddenly an alarm screeched through the complex. The police told everyone to rush into the next room. In there we found Dad who had no answer for what was happening. Very quickly we boarded the plane then waited. Through the window I watched another plane land. It was odd somehow; longer and skinnier than any plane I had ever seen on television. Dad said it was a Soviet plane and we figured out what happened. The Soviet plane was full of passengers who would need the space we were in during our inspection. They were probably important men from Russia, Dad said, men Castro needed.

We got lucky, but a lot of people didn't. At best the inspection was embarrassing for those involved; at worst, inhumane. We spent at most twenty minutes sitting in the still plane, but it felt like hours. We were so close now. The pilot said a few words over the intercom and then began take off. I was pulled deep into my seat as the plane picked up speed. I had never been on a plane before and I wasn't sure what was normal. I guess I expected something smoother. I closed my eyes while the plane covered ground across the runway. Finally we left the pavement, and I opened my eyes. I looked out the window again and watched the airport shrink and then fade away entirely. I saw the city of Havana as I had never seen it. From above the city looked prosperous and peaceful. For a second, I wondered why we were leaving. The city melted into the countryside and the countryside into the sea. Cuba was behind us and there was no turning back.

12

For nearly an hour I stared into the water below. It was only a Gulf, but it was endless enough to fascinate and still enough to bore. The wavering blue lulled my eyes shut though I fought the urge. I didn't want to miss the journey sleeping. I settled somewhere in between, neither awake enough to smell the unveiling of our flight meal nor asleep enough to imagine I was somewhere else.

"Would you like a sandwich?"

"What?" I rubbed stars from my eyes. I looked out the window once more. It was still there, blue and still. I rubbed my eyes again. I saw a tan girl with a cart full of food.

"A sandwich?" She held it out to me. Next to me Joaquin was already halfway through his. I took the sandwich from the attendant. Without saying anything she handed me a bottle of orange juice, a cookie, even a magazine. After she gave Dad the same treatment she moved on to the next row. Across the plane another flight attendant, just as pretty, did the same.

"Can you believe it? She brought *me* food. I didn't even have to wait in line," Mom spoke to no one in particular, but we all heard. Dad's eyes scanned the cabin as she spoke. There were certainly passengers aboard who would not appreciate the words, though

71

she spoke no lies. I hadn't tasted orange juice in years or bitten into a respectable sandwich. I should have savored the cookie a little longer. Mom had more to say, but kept it inside.

We followed the same route as the Conquistadors 400 years before, except our journey would last hours, not weeks. Just like them, we sought a new world with golden opportunities. We landed in Merida, near the northwest tip of the Yucatan Peninsula. We didn't leave our seats as crewman refueled the plane. Had it taken longer, I may have realized that the next time we landed I would be further from the sea than I had ever been. In twenty minutes we were back in the air, pointed toward Mexico City.

I could still see the sea below me for another few hours, but eventually it was replaced by patches of dark green and brown. As we approached the site of the ancient Aztec city of Tenoch-titlan, the pilot announced on the radio that the airport was too crowded and we could not land. The plane would have to bypass the airport and fly around in circles until the pilot received new instructions.

"Is this normal?" my brother asked me.

"Yes." I had no idea, but for a time I believed myself. The minutes passed until well-dressed men paced down the aisle, demanding answers from flight attendants. An hour ticked by and we heard no news, only an announcement that the pilot would be turning off the air conditioning to save fuel. Another circle, this time sweaty and humid. Another, this time a young boy vomited in the last row, and the dominos fell. Another boy couldn't hold his lunch, then gasps, scurrying flight attendants and an atrocious smell. "This is definitely not normal."

We finally began a descent, and after fifteen minutes of holding our breath, the cabin doors opened. We were safe on the runway, but for some reason surrounded by ambulances and fire trucks. Before we could ask why, airport officials stormed into the cabin yelling for us to remain in our seats. They confiscated Cuban media, row by row. They scoured each seat for anything that even resembled a newspaper or magazine. I turned over the magazine I received a few hours before. I hadn't even opened it.

The officials finished their hunt, and we were able to disembark. Dad asked an attendant why the ambulances were there. She looked both ways like she was about to cross a street, and then spoke softly. They were there for us, our plane. Our delay was due to faulty landing gear; our circling was really an attempt to buy time to fix the problem. It worked, but it was miserable. Not as miserable, though, as the alternative. Had the problem not been fixed, we would have been making a belly landing on the runway, hence the ambulances. That could have made for a short adventure.

When we landed, our day did not get any less weird. A newspaper reporter stood in the lobby of the terminal when we entered. He asked for a moment of our time to ask us questions about Cuba. Eager for a chance to tell the world what was going on in Castro's Cuba, Dad agreed. We waited while Dad and the reporter spoke in the corner. Dad stood a full foot taller than the reporter. He was a chubby man with a thick mustache who hardly looked up from the notepad that he jotted on. When they were done, I asked my Dad what they talked about.

"He asked me what it was like in Cuba."

"What did you tell him?"

"The truth." Food shortages, disappearing cousins, invasive community leaders? I wasn't sure which truth he referred to, but plenty was newsworthy. The reporter claimed he would have a story in the next day's paper. Dad looked forward to seeing himself quoted.

Our late arrival gave us a new difficulty. We were supposed to change flights in Mexico City and head towards Kingston, Jamaica, but our midair circling made that impossible. The next Jamaica-bound flight did not leave for a week, so our pit stop in Mexico City would now be a weeklong stay. The Mexican custom officials took our passports and told us to come back in a week. At the time I had no idea why we had to go through all of this trouble. Why couldn't we just go straight to Wisconsin? I asked. Dad answered with a rant about Mexico, Cuba and everything wrong with the world. I was able to gather that the Mexican government did not want Cubans settling in Mexico. Taking our passports made it much harder for us to decide to stay there for the long term. Mexico wanted us gone to be someone else's problem.

Luckily an old friend of my father's, Mr. Oliva, came to the airport to say hello. He was Dad's client many years before and was just planning on greeting us as we went on our way. When we saw him, we told him of our dilemma. We were stuck here for a week. Mr. Oliva absolutely saved the day. Without hesitation, he took us to his home for lunch where we met his wife and stepdaughter, and I was introduced to Mexican cuisine. Mrs. Oliva offered us *tortillas*. To us a *tortilla* was a kind of omelet, so I was a bit confused when she loaded it with beans, beef and vegetables. When she handed the finished product to me, I called it a sandwich. The Olivas laughed and said it was a *taco*.

I didn't mind being wrong, but being laughed at by his daughter, Camilla, was upsetting. She was about my age with dark, curly hair, very bright eyes and an ever-present smile. When she finally stopped giggling, it didn't take long for her to find a reason to start again. First it was our confusion with the food, and then she grew fascinated with our accents. I couldn't say a word without her reacting. She said our accents were so musical. This startled me. Mexicans and Cubans spoke the same language and basically looked the same, how could she keep finding differences between us? In time though, we would find that we had much more in common than not.

After a mid-afternoon lunch (due to our late arrival), I settled in the living room where Mr. Oliva grilled Dad for first-hand knowledge of Cuba. Mom stayed in the kitchen and washed dishes long after Mrs. Oliva told her to stop. Again we found ourselves at the mercy of others, and Mom was committed to being as little of a burden as possible. It kept her busy.

Mr. Oliva left Cuba, where he grew up, years before, and was very curious to know what the conditions were on the island. Dad gave him a slightly more detailed account than he told the journalist a few hours prior. I drifted in and out of sleep, so I don't remember much. I was awake when Dad asked him about Mexico's policy about Cubans entering Mexico. This was new to me, so I stood up to listen. Mr. Oliva told us to be very skeptical of Mexico's "super-ficial friendship" with Cuba. He said Mexico was speaking out of both sides of its mouth. On the one hand they needed to keep a healthy relationship with the United States; but, by befriending Cuba, they gained "symbolic distance" from the U.S. and satisfied socialist groups in Mexico.

I was fascinated by the topic because it was the first time I heard about Cuban events from an outside perspective. I had no idea that what happened on a small Caribbean island could shape policies of enormous nations like Mexico and the U.S. In a strange way, I was proud that Cuba mattered – even if took a communist takeover for outsiders to pay attention.

Camilla grew tired of the conversation quickly and stepped out into the backyard. I followed. I'd had my fill of politics. Outside, I immediately noticed another difference between Cuba and Mexico. It was cold, much colder than it ever got in Cuba, especially in July. Camilla laughed again when I told her I was cold. "It's summer," she said in-between giggles.

"Exactly, why is it so cold!"

"We're high above the sea and surrounded by mountains and volcanoes, maybe that's why." I was impressed and shocked she stopped laughing long enough to say it. It made sense; I had never been this high above sea level. I hadn't thought about it, but the plane was taking us uphill as well as west. I asked her a hundred more questions about Mexico and she did the same about Cuba. I told her about Mr. Bello and his rally at our home. She gasped, put her hand on my shoulder and offered soothing words. I really wasn't upset about that anymore, but I didn't say anything to stop her.

Hours later, Mr. Oliva drove us to a hotel in the city. The drive took about a half hour and was full of memorable sightings of what a non-communist nation looked like. First though, we saw something unforgettably strange. Before we had even left the Oliva's neighborhood, I saw a man walking a dog on the side of the road. The dog had a light bulb attached to its tail. As it wagged back and forth, the flicker of light followed. I pointed it out to my brother and he erupted with laughter.

Mr. Oliva couldn't explain it. "That's not strange because its foreign." he said, "That's just strange. I've never seen that before." He was laughing, too. Mr. Oliva was concerned that our only impression of Mexico City would be the quirky dog, so he started pointing out buildings and landmarks with increasing frequency. Joaquin, Lidia, and I couldn't get over the dog though. We demanded to drive back until Mom said to stop asking. When we had finally calmed down, Lidia ruined it.

"Where does the battery go?" Lidia asked. Even Mom laughed.

In the city we saw giant department stores that no longer existed in Cuba. Mom told me that when I was very young I was in *The Encanto* (the store that burned down) before it was ruined, but I couldn't remember that. We saw a Ford dealership and a GM plant, restaurants with lines out their doors, grocery stores where you could chose what to buy. The trip was an eye-opening display of commercialism for me, although I learned it comes at a cost. We encountered the worst traffic jam I had ever been a part of, but Mr. Oliva called it normal. Cuba didn't have traffic jams; we simply didn't have enough cars for that. Cuba's lack of cars also meant I had never encountered air pollution. The congested streets full of trucks exhaling fumes gave me a headache. My impatience made it worse.

We finally made it to the hotel, and it didn't take me long to hit the pillow. We had a small room with two queen-sized beds in it. My brother, sister and I piled into one, my parents into the other. I was dead tired, but lay awake for a while. Joaquin rolled over every five minutes, Lidia kicked like she was drowning. I wasn't comfortable, but that's not all that kept me up. I woke up that morning in my home country and fell asleep in a cold, new place full of sights I didn't understand. My exhaustion could not keep my mind from wandering through familiar Cuban towns and congested Mexican streets.

I could hear my Mom stirring. She wasn't asleep. At the Oliva's she put on her charming face, gossiped with Mrs. Oliva and did her best to repay their kindness. She filled every empty cup and washed every plate in spite of Mrs. Oliva's protests that we were guests. She hated how dependent we were on others, but there was no way around it. While others were watching she was strong, but now in the dark room I finally sensed her frustration. Many times sleep crawled close, but scurried off at the sound of my mother's sighs.

13

"Look at this." I opened my eyes to an unraveled newspaper. A tan finger pointed to a headline: "Cubans Survive Escape, Barely." It took no more than a few seconds to remember where I was. Dad tapped the headline one more time. I rubbed my eyes and started reading. The article described the scene at the airport, paramedics prepping for a belly landing, pale passengers thankful to get off a vomit-filled plane. I knew the ending of course; crisis averted. Cuban refugees complete the first step of their exodus. But the article quoted a Mr. Castro with no relation to Fidel. The quote described widespread dissent in Cuba, food shortages and an imprisoned cousin.

"This is what you said." I said it like he didn't already know. He laughed before moving the article on to Joaquin who was still sleeping. "Why did they change your name?"

"Canto, Castro. It's only a small change."

"But it's *his* name."

"Yes, how poetic. Castro escapes Castro. Easy to remember, too. Maybe they sell a few more newspapers today."

"But–"

"Or perhaps you should be thankful. Do you really want Castro to know what you think of him? We have the same name, he might have blamed you."

"But we left."

"We're not so far, you don't think he has agents in Mexico?" He was still laughing. I hadn't figured out what was funny, but I laughed, too. Then Joaquin's confused face turned into a grin and his laughter joined ours. Lidia walked into the room from the bathroom demanding to know what was so funny, but joined in when she heard us fumble to give her an answer. She leapt on the bed then on to Dad's back as Mom walked into the room carrying pastries.

The noise startled her and for half a moment she glared as us with concern. We quieted as if we were doing something wrong, but a smile took her lips, a real smile, not a prop. It wavered at first, afraid to take root, until Lidia's giggling conquered every other noise in the room. Then it took form and hung around for a while.

• • •

Not only did Mr. Oliva feed us and loan us money to survive, but he also made it his personal mission to ensure we enjoyed ourselves and learned a few things on our unplanned vacation to Mexico City. He picked us up around noon the next day and said he was taking us to a very famous park called *Chapultepec*. It was old, he said, it was there before the Spanish, even the Aztecs. More than a thousand years ago a strange people called the Toltec believed the site to be sacred. After them, the spot was a resort for Aztec nobility. It spanned miles and miles, was full of museums, a zoo, even a royal castle.

"Royal? Mexico has a king?"

"Once long ago. An Emperor, actually. Emperor Maximilian I from Austria with his wife Carlota, a princess of Belgium."

"They ruled here?"

"The history is complicated. In the 1860s, Mexico was under constant unrest, war, revolutions, governments all over the country, each calling themselves the official government." That sounded familiar. "Napoleon in France wanted an ally in the Americas."

"Napoleon Bonaparte?" I knew that name, and I made sure he knew it.

"No the other one. His nephew, Napoleon III." Now I was confused. "Some members of the Mexican parliament thought it was in the best interest of Mexico to gain French protection and give the throne to a monarch of Napoleon's choosing for stability. The problem was that most Mexicans didn't want someone from Europe showing up and telling them what to do. Who would?

"So in 1864, here came Maximilian and Carlota, full of good intentions. He tried to help the poor and unite Mexico, but he never stood a chance. The other government overthrew him and killed him. His wife fled to Europe, but he refused to leave his people. He was brave if nothing else. Oh, he built this avenue." I looked around. I hadn't noticed how big the street was. Six lanes wide, lined with well-decorated streetlights and skyscrapers taller than any I had ever seen. *El Paseo de la Reforma* took us straight into the park. Mr. Oliva led us into the park that never seemed to end until we stood in front of a castle that belonged in a fairy tale.

Arches, three times my height, lined the façade. At the peak of the three central most arches, engraved stone faces of past heroes watched over the entrances. Tall, circular towers stood at the corners of the building. Once men stood guard on those towers, but there was no longer an enemy to watch for. The castle stood on a hill protected by a forest that extended in every direction until it faded into the downtown beyond. Never had I seen a structure so permanent.

An Emperor lived here once, sent by another Emperor from the other side of the world to rule. Emperor Maximilian I, who brought good intentions to a country full of people that didn't trust or want him. Was that worse than a president that the people didn't trust or want? I wasn't sure. Castro is at least Cuban. But then again that's what made it so tragic. He imprisoned and suppressed his own countrymen. President, emperor, king, prime minister: the name isn't what was important, but what the ruler does with that power.

80

Inside we saw the royal dining room and the magnificent bedroom of Empress Carlota. The castle no longer served a role in the government, and had been turned into the Museum of National History. Portraits covered the walls of long corridors that led to rooms full of artifacts from the past, Spanish rifles, Aztec headdresses. The history was interesting for a while, but when we entered the mirror room my capacity for learning was transplanted. Some mirrors made me look like a three-foot-tall pumpkin. Others made me a giant, although a very frail one. Joaquin and I raced up and down the hall, watching ourselves transform from dwarfs to aliens to mutants.

Hours later we were back in the car and exhausted. I wanted nothing more than to go back to the hotel and lie down, but Mom wouldn't have it. We were going shopping. We left the same way we came in, on Maximilian's famous avenue, and then made our way through the congested city. I kept seeing the same few posters in the windows of shops or on light posts. Some were the same colors as the Mexican flag. Others were blue and white. I couldn't make out the words. "What are those posters?" I asked Mr. Oliva.

"Political posters. There's an election in a few days."

"But there are two of them."

"Of course. The ones that look like the Mexican flag are for the PRI, *El Partido Revolucionario Instucional*. The party that always wins. The others are for the PAN, *El Partido Acción Nacional*[6]. They're more conservative and powerful only in the north. The PAN thinks they can win this year. I doubt it."

I knew what elections were, but I had never seen one. Castro said he would hold them at the beginning of his reign, but they never came. It was interesting to see different posters though. In Cuba all the posters had one message: "All Hail Fidel." There were no other parties but his.

We made it to a giant store called "Sears." It had everything: TV's, radios, couches, clothes. We could have filled our whole house, if we had one, without ever having to go to a different store. I couldn't believe what I was seeing. The customers paid with

6   The party names translate roughly to The Party of Revolutionary Institutions and The Party of National Action. The titles are about as ambiguous as Democrat and Republican.

money instead of ration cards and could get as much of anything as they wanted. If a customer wanted a mattress, he had thirty to choose from. Mom walked through aisles and aisles of dresses and blouses. We had no money to buy anything, but I think it made her stronger just to see that stores like this still existed. She was back in the old Cuba for an hour or two.

In the front of the store there was a small food court. Mr. Oliva treated Joaquin, Lidia and me to delicious, chocolate milkshakes. I hadn't tasted the refreshing sweetness of a milkshake in years, since milk became a rare commodity. I finished it without stopping to breathe. When all I held was an empty cup, I attacked Joaquin's shake with a spoon.

"No way," he said as he put himself on the opposite side of the bench we were sitting on.

"Come on, just a bite!"

"You should have eaten slower. Do you know who would have loved this? Tony." He was right. Tony, our plump friend who umped our baseball games, complained often about missing snacks, candy bars and, mostly, ice cream. Tony would not be having a milkshake for a long time, if ever. Neither would Carlos or Ramon. A country with barely enough food to feed its people had no room for milkshakes. I looked around the store. My old friends had none of this. Then I thought of Ignacio, he had even less. I sat on the bench for a long while feeling guilty that I had the chance to eat a milkshake. Nothing about it was fair. I sulked for a minute until I thought of Mr. Bello. He wouldn't be eating a milkshake anytime soon either. I felt a little better.

14

studied a menu a few mornings later at a café. I knew the language, but the words were unfamiliar. Cubans and Mexicans use the same words about 90% of the times, but for some reason they have their names for foods, and we have ours. Dad ordered coffee and toast. He clearly wasn't in the mood for experimenting. I ran my finger down the list of items. *Rollo de Canela. Canela* I knew, cinnamon. But *rollo*, roll, what did that mean? There was only one way to find out. After one look at it, I was not disappointed. Joaquin felt the same way about his gamble, a sugar covered pastry called a *garibaldi*. I caught him eying my roll a few times, and we negotiated a trade.

Dad didn't so much as peek at the array of treats on the table. He hid his face behind an open newspaper, looking up only to ask the waitress to refill his coffee. I could see the front page of the newspaper where his face should have been. It was Election Day. That must be what he's reading about. Maybe he had seen elections before Castro and Batista, but that would have been years before. Finally he spoke, "Article after article critiquing the candidates and the election process. I would love nothing more than to have an election to criticize in Cuba."

He must not have realized he said the words out loud. When he poked his head out from behind the newspaper he seemed surprised to see eyes staring back at him. Realizing he had smothered the mood, he changed the subject to something he knew would distract Joaquin and me. He folded the paper to reveal a picture of a dark skinned baseball player wearing a navy cap with a red "T" across the front.

"You've heard of my cousin I see? Great player, you can listen to him play in a few days." Mr. Oliva had just arrived and was standing over my shoulder looking down at the picture in front of me. Dad let out a chuckle while Joaquin and I exchanged confused looks. We were missing something. I read the caption of the picture: Cuban All Star Tony Oliva hopes to keep up his recent hot hitting at Tuesday's All-Star Game.

"Is he really your—" Mr. Oliva's face gave away the answer. Disappointed, I turned back to the paper. I read through the names of every player who had made the All Star game. A few I knew. Most were new to me. Following American baseball was a lot easier before Castro took over Cuban baseball. In the past, the Cuban players in America were revered in Cuba. Now American and Cuban baseball were two separate universes. That ended most of the interest in American baseball, but Castro's nationalization of the Cuban media was its deathblow. Those who cared had no way of following the game.

Nonetheless, the prospect of getting to experience Major League Baseball, even if it was only by radio, was exciting. I read through the names again as if I would be quizzed on them in America. Baseball would be the one thing I could count on there. Despite all the differences between Cuba and America, we had that in common. Dad took the paper from me and asked Mr. Oliva a hundred questions about the election. Quickly I grew disinterested and turned my attention back to the treats on my plate.

After a few minutes of chatting, Dad had enough. He snapped up and said he was going to see this election for himself. Whoever wanted to join him could do so. Mom, sister and brother were uninterested. My alternative was to spend the day trapped in an undersized hotel with most of the family, so I needed little persuading. Mr. Oliva offered to drive and once again be our tour guide. Our day was set; I was to spend the day experiencing democracy. Before we could go, there was one small matter to attend to: the check. The waiter handed Dad the check and he set it on the table. I snuck a peek to feel like an adult. 74 *pesos*, how could that be?

Dad chuckled after seeing the shock on my face. "Eight Mexican *pesos* equals one dollar." That helped a little, but I had never heard of a Mexican *peso*, in Cuba they were just *pesos*. "One dollar and one Cuban *peso* are worth the same value. They've been on par for a long time." I had always assumed that a dollar and a *peso* were the same thing with different names, like water and *agua*. But they were different somehow, and a Cuban *peso* and a Mexican *peso* were different too. It was starting to make sense, but one question still bugged me.

"Why can't Mexico and Cuba use the same *peso*?"

"The same reason why they have elections and we don't. Every country has its own government and they decide the rules. Mexico has its own banks and its own currency because that's what the government decided. When you change countries, the money changes and sometimes the rules too."

This conversation was a perfect prelude to a day spent experiencing democracy. It continued in the car with Dad offering his insights of banking practices and currency exchange. I understood very little of it and after a minute or two even Mr. Oliva seemed bored. Dad hadn't been a banker in a couple years, but his passion was indestructible. He needed a good money talk, even if it was only with himself.

Mr. Oliva took us on a thirty-minute drive deep into downtown. I still wasn't used to the sea of taxis or the noise of the streets. Every few seconds I heard a cab blow its horn, unless a large truck was nearby overpowering every other noise with its motor. We zigzagged through the traffic until we were, once again, surrounded by skyscrapers. We stopped at a pay lot a short walk from what Mr. Oliva assured us would be a very busy polling center.

He wasn't lying. We turned the corner and saw a line stretching from the front doors of some sort of community center. Men and women wearing shirts of the competing political parties paced up and down the lines. They passed out flyers and hung placards on light posts. Despite the mass numbers, the line was moving. From another door, men and women hurried back to their lives now that their civic duty was complete. What struck me most was the diversity. Waiting to vote were gray-haired men in suits and young women dressed like it was a Saturday night. The voters differed dramatically in wealth. A look at their clothes was all it took to predict their social class. We walked into the polling center and saw just how long the line stretched. It continued through the lobby and into another room that was off limits to us.

"Are you going to vote?" I said to Dad and Mr. Oliva.

"I can't," Dad responded. "Only the citizens of Mexico can decide what happens in Mexico."

"And I've only been here a few years," Mr. Oliva chimed in, "I'm not a citizen either." I was disappointed that we were only spectators.

"I can't believe how organized this is. It must require a lot of planning," Dad said just as a toddler sprinted by from across the lobby. A woman left her place in line to chase down her untamed child.

"You call this organized?" Mr. Oliva said after a laugh. The woman walked back by us clutching her frantic child. She gave us an embarrassed look and made her way back into line. Just then a short, middle-aged man walked into the lobby. His hair was uncombed, and his clothes were full of rips and stains and smelled like his outfit had been pieced together from trashcans. He looked at the line, then at us, then back to the line. An aide walked over to him and asked him if he needed help. He wanted to vote, he told the aide. The aide led him outside and pointed to the end of the line just as we were exiting. The aide watched the man take a few steps towards the line then walked back inside just as the dirty man turned back around. He watched in horror as the door closed behind the aide.

Lost once again, he looked as us with his arms held wide. "Whom do I vote for?" Mr. Oliva motioned toward him. Probably

86

to tell him it was his choice. That's the whole point. But before he could say anything a man handing out flyers jumped in front of Mr. Oliva.

"Do you see these colors?" The man held up a red, white and green flyer, the colors found on the Mexican flag. "A vote for PRI is a vote for Mexico." He handed the prospective voter a flier and gave him a pat on the shoulder. I thought of what Mr. Oliva said about PRI, they always win. I wonder why. Dad must have had the same thought.

"Is that democracy?" Unsurprisingly, we awoke the next morning to news of another victory by PRI.

• • •

"The bed is shaking!" It was a little later than midnight, but I wasn't quite asleep. Mom would sometimes get dizzy spells, so I didn't give too much thought to her words. But, then I felt it. Joaquin, who was lying right next to me, leapt out of bed. I looked around just as Dad flipped a light switch and watched a lamp shake its way off of a shelf. Voices grew louder in the stairwell outside the room. A woman screamed, then my sister did. I sat up and touched my feet to the shaky ground. I put a hand on the wall to steady myself. What on earth was going on?

Outside a voice I recognized grew louder than the others. It was the clerk from the front desk of the hotel. "It's only a *temblor*. Don't worry. The building is safe. It will soon pass." Only a *temblor*! How do you tell a Cuban that it was only a *temblor*? I had only ever heard of earthquakes in movies and they never ended well. Later Mr. Oliva would explain to us that a *temblor* was a minor earthquake, what we might call just a tremor, and a *terremoto* is a major one, but that wouldn't bring much relief. An earthquake is an earthquake if you've never been in one before.

It was over in a minute, but it felt like an hour. My sister kept screaming. Joaquin curled in a corner and hugged his knees. "Castro!" Mom screamed. "*Castro tu imbécil!* Oh, that you had never

87

been born!" This was her way of dealing with a situation she had no control over. She bottled up all her emotions and directed them at Castro. It's actually a very good stress management technique if you ever want to try it. Castro was responsible for plenty of evil in the world, but he couldn't shake the earth. That didn't matter though. To Mom every hardship we would encounter for the next few years was his fault. We should have been back on the still island living quiet, happy lives. Instead, we were in an earthquake.

Dad worked to calm down Mom as I turned my attention to Lidia. I don't think she could hear my words over the sound of footsteps outside or Mom's screaming, but it wouldn't matter. It ended as abruptly as it started. The screams quieted, and Dad walked around picking objects off the floor. Shards from the lamp's bulb lay all over the floor, so he went off to find a broom to sweep it up. He came back with the hotel manager who ensured that we were just fine. We were, I suppose. But that wasn't something that we had prepared for. Culture shock, money confusion, cold weather, that was to be expected, but it would have required an incredible feat of the imagination for a Cuban to plan for an earthquake.

Sleep did not come easy the rest of the night for anyone. Anytime someone got out of bed and stepped on the floor I snapped awake. Even the tiny vibrations of a footstep alarmed me. The bed shook in my mind. The same way you might feel like you're still on a boat hours after you've been on dry land. It was hardest for Lidia. I don't think she had ever even heard of an earthquake. To her it must have felt like the world was ending.

The next day it was all we could talk about. We didn't leave the room except to eat. The earthquake caused some damage around the city and made the traffic that much worse, but that's not the only reason why I didn't want to leave. I didn't trust the earth to stay still. Better to stay in the room where we were safe. I can't imagine anything worse than being caught in something like this on the street. It took a while to get over the fear that an earthquake would surely strike at any time.

Our last days in Mexico did provide one major distraction. We heard the Major League All-Star Game on an old, static-ridden radio in our hotel room. It was odd listening to the announcer describe players who I had never heard of, and even stranger to imagine that in a short time we would be in that country. Tony Oliva started for the American League in right field. It didn't matter that I had only heard of him a few days before. I cheered for him like he was my childhood hero. Not just because he was Cuban, but also because he was a Cuban thriving in America. He made the All-Star game as a rookie and would even go on to win the American League Rookie of the Year that season. He didn't play particularly well in that game, but it didn't matter. I had a new idol. Besides him, the only other thing that I remember from that game is Johnny Callision, whoever he was, won the game for the National League with a walk off homer. When the game ended, the United States did not seem so foreign.

15

Our unplanned vacation in Mexico had to come to an end. What was supposed to be a change of flight turned into an education in culture, politics and natural disasters, not to mention a really good time. Just one week after our frightful landing experience, we were back at the Mexican Airport ready to finally embark toward our original destination, Jamaica. Why Jamaica? For starters, Jamaica was close. Jamaica and Cuba had developed a working relationship over the years. In the days before Castro, Jamaicans could acquire work visas to work sugar fields in Cuba. Jamaicans came to Cuba for a few months, worked the fields, then went home with some cash. Maybe Jamaicans felt like they owed Cubans or sympathized with our situation, I'm not really sure. The main reason was that Jamaica, unlike Mexico, had no restrictions in place for Cuban refugees to apply to enter the United States. Mexico and many other countries didn't want to get caught in the middle of a dispute between the United States and Cuba, so they avoided the whole situation. Jamaica clearly didn't care. Thousands of Cubans took the route through Jamaica on the way to the United States.

As we waited at the airport in Mexico, I noticed we would be flying on a plane called a Comet. I was a plane nut back then, so I was ecstatic to see one. The Comet had the jet engines close to the body of the plane instead of towards the end of the wings like most planes. I tried to explain this to my family, but none of them seemed to care. Once we boarded the plane I found a new reason to be excited. The flight attendants were, once again, young and beautiful. One walked over to us and asked if we were doing OK. I most certainly was. I asked her about the Comet, and she was very impressed that I knew the name. I made sure Joaquin heard her praise, but I can't say knowing the name of an airplane ever got me attention from a girl again. I asked her if we would be flying over Cuba. We weren't, but I already knew that. She pointed to the window to my left and said it was out there somewhere, too far to see. It must have occurred to her then that we were fleeing Cubans because all the sudden her face grew cold. She patted me on the shoulder and wished me luck on our journey. Our last flight was a disaster, but this one was looking much better already.

As we took off I realized what Mr. Oliva's explanation for Mexico's air pollution meant. He said giant mountains surrounded the city and trapped the smog. The mountains made for terrible conditions on the ground, but from up there they were simply breathtaking. After a moment of awe I watched them sink. About 90 minutes later we were over the blue waters of the Caribbean. Even though I knew I wouldn't see Cuba, I found myself staring out the window the attendant pointed too. I was able to see a few other islands including the Cayman Islands. Their beauty was apparent, even at 30,000 feet of altitude.

It didn't take long after landing in Kingston, Jamaica, to discover that this stop would be a journey of its own. Outside we were greeted by a group of men from the Cuban Refugee Center who gave us a ride to the Center in an old van. Dad must have given them a heads up of our arrival. On the way there, I saw sights I had never seen before. Every bus we passed had grown men literally hanging off the back of it. I don't know if it was full or if that was a sneaky way of catching a ride without paying for it. The roads that were paved were cracked and looked ready to crumble under the weight of the van. The streets were littered with piles of trash. Intersections had no traffic signals, creating a free-for-all among the sputtering heaps of rust that they called cars. Some of the buildings we passed looked vaguely modern, but for the most part Kingston seemed to be stuck in a time capsule.

Most shocking of all, very skinny, inadequately dressed children occupied the street corners. I watched with disbelief as groups of four or five children mobbed pedestrians with their palms held open. The sight broke our hearts, but we had nothing to offer. Our situation was not nearly as desperate, but we were dependent on the aid of others as well. Our belongings were in Cuba. We were able to get our hands on some money in Mexico, donations from family members who were already in America, but that money needed to be saved for our eventual flight to America. The starving kids provided me perspective. There are worse things in life than not being able to drink a milkshake.

The Refugee Center was less than inspiring. It was full of small rooms where refugees could stay temporarily, but it was very obvious that the center had no vacancies. The center was divided in half. One side of the building housed men, the other side, women. The only families I saw were sitting around waiting for news or food or hope like we were. The center offered services for escaping Cubans like us because it would be some time before we could leave Jamaica. We had to apply for entry into the United States, and then, once again, wait for approval. Somehow, the thousands of Cubans who showed up on the shores of their Caribbean neighbors with nothing had to be housed and fed.

Dad went to speak with the director of the center, a local priest who looked just like Cassius Clay (the boxer who later changed his name to Muhammad Ali), about securing a room for us. The rest of us sat in an all purpose room that was being prepared for use as a dining hall. The Center was buzzing with activity. In a distant room an infant cried and cried, while a small crew of workers set up tables and chairs for the eventual dinner rush. The most prominent sounds were the shouts of men waiting to use the shower.

Dad returned with the news we were expecting. The Center was full, but there were a few inns nearby that may have a room for us. He went off to find out and we stayed at the Center. He was gone for several hours, but returned with good tidings. He found a room, but it would not be comfortable. None of us cared. We hadn't been comfortable all day.

The next day our situation improved slightly. Dad found a man named Mr. Creeks who was willing to rent us a spare room, much more appropriately sized, for the rest of our stay. Mr. Creeks spoke enough Spanish to communicate with us, but not enough to say anything meaningful. He was one of the Jamaicans who used to spend his summers in Cuba working the fields with a permit. Castro's ascent to power left him without that annual opportunity to help feed his family, so he had nearly as much animosity for Castro as we did. Communication was impossible with his wife, an extremely warm and courteous woman, for she did not speak a word of Spanish. We met her and their two teenage sons, Donovan and Noah, that same afternoon and were greeted with a very welcomed warm, home-cooked meal.

The initial excitement of finding a reliable place to settle was quickly replaced by dread when I saw the size of the room. The five of us spent the next two months living in a single room about the size of my bedroom in Cuba. We had a full-sized bed where my parents and Lidia slept, and Joaquin and I were left the floor. I got used to it eventually, but the first nights were hard. Literally, the floor was hard. I lay awake for hours holding a tiny short wave radio Dad bought in Mexico. I listened to the Voice of America, and then scanned the airwaves for anything to serve as a lullaby. I picked up an overnight show for truck drivers called *Radio Caracol* from Colombia. The show played music I never heard before, mixed with commentary on topics that bored me, but that was the point. For the first of many nights I fell asleep to traffic reports from Colombia.

• • •

We spent the early part of that year waiting for a telegram. Summer would be only slightly different. We were powerless visitors in Jamaica with no plans or ambitions – except leaving. If it wasn't for the occasional sight of a child picking through a trashcan or a dilapidated shack, we might have dissolved into despair. But it was impossible to feel bad about my life when I was surrounded by such poverty.

The only similarity to Cuba was the climate. Everything else was unusual. I spent most of the day out in a garden in Mr. Creeks's backyard under the perfect sun with my brother and sister. We had no activities, no commitments, nothing. Our entertainment was running around outside, playing a made up version of baseball with a makeshift ball, a rock wrapped in a sock. Donavon and Noah helped to quell the boredom by filling the house with music they called "ska." The music was upbeat and made for dancing, and we saw plenty of that from our host family. Mrs. Creeks could not sit still when the music was playing and took the hand of whoever was nearest and forced them to join her fun. The rest of the family clapped to the rhythm and encouraged the dancers.

Of our two-month stay in Jamaica I remember very little. Most days were no different than the one before it. Afternoons in the garden and late nights with a radio pressed to my ear. Counting down the minutes until we were out of that place and to our final destination took up the bulk of my time. Occasionally Joaquin's antics would provide a break in the routine. Donavon and Joaquin didn't exactly see eye to eye, and often times Donavon gave Joaquin a look that suggested that Joaquin was very lucky to be six years younger. It reached a breaking point one day when Joaquin and I chanced upon Donavon and a giggling lady friend of his sitting on the patio together. We watched for a few minutes trying to get a good look of her. We were not disappointed. For minutes it was the same thing, he would whisper in her ear, then she would laugh and put her head on his shoulder. In a perfect homage to Raul, Joaquin turned to me and said, "Watch this." He had seen enough.

Quietly he situated himself very near the teenage lovebirds, close enough that he could clearly hear her laughter. Then he started singing the words, "I love you just the way you are," the chorus of a song called "Rag Doll." The day before we had overheard Donavon signing the words of that song, a big hit that summer by a band called The Four Seasons, quite passionately when he thought he was alone. He was even using a shoe for a microphone. The music was so loud that he could not hear us erupting with laughter in the next room. As soon as Donavon heard Joaquin's singing he leapt to his feet with a look of horror. Now aware of Joaquin's plan, I joined his production. When we reached the end of the chorus we looked at each other nervously then repeated it, neither of us knew the rest of the words.

Of all of the ways Donavon could have handled that situation he picked the absolute worst. He started screaming obscenities at a 12-year-old and a 10-year-old in front of a girl he was trying to dazzle. She didn't have a clue who we were, and she obviously wasn't around for his private concerto with the shoe, so he could have given her any explanation of who these two lighter skinned, raggedy looking kids were, and why they were singing that particular song. Instead his actions appalled her, and she stormed out of the house. The relations between Donavon and the two of us took a turn for the worst that day. Even though, as Joaquin pointed out often, it was really his own temper that ruined his chances with his friend. I doubt Donavon ever came that close again to striking a child.

After that, Joaquin and I kept our distance from Donavon and Noah. Joaquin was all for starting more trouble, but I reminded him we were guests in their home. We got all the entertainment we could out of our makeshift baseball, but not surprisingly after a few weeks of heavy use it met its end. The sock deteriorated leaving only a rock, and we weren't about to play ball with a rock. We had no replacement socks, because we only had a few sets of clothes each. It was with great reluctance that Mom had let us sacrifice a withered pair in the first place. The other sock in the pair was nowhere to be found and even Joaquin knew it was a terrible idea to ask Donavon or Noah to donate a sock to our cause. It seemed our time there was about to get even more boring.

But we were rescued by a man named Moises and the charitable work of the Cuban Jewish community, which, believe it or not, exists and was in full force during Cuba's moment of crisis. Moises was a childhood friend of my father and a proud member of the Jewish faith. He and Dad had not seen each other in decades but were reacquainted in Jamaica. Moises, like us, was waiting to leave the country, but, unlike us, the generous work of his Jewish brethren gave him a resource for food, clothing and shelter that was unavailable to us. Moises though, after visiting our temporary home, decided that he could and should do something. He told my father, Joaquin and me to come with him to downtown Kingston, but he was ambiguous on the details.

We hopped onto a crowded bus and made the commute downtown. The ride was terrifying. The bus made a piercing roar as it struggled to climb even the slightest hills. The bus was overrun with a repugnant smell that Dad said was what twenty people with no running water smell like. The smell choked me, but I tried hard to not seem insensitive. Several of the passengers on the bus gave us curious glances. We obviously weren't natives, but we weren't tourists either. Tourists don't get anywhere near those busses.

We passed more children on the street, but it no longer fazed me. That was the saddest part. The sights of poverty were a part of the scenery, like the crumbling buildings and potholes. We exited the bus right in front of a movie theatre, and I will never forget what film it was showing, Elvis' *Fun in Acapulco*. I couldn't believe he was popular enough to make his way into deteriorating downtown Kingston. From there we walked a few blocks until we were in front of a very inconspicuous warehouse. As we approached Moises turned to us and said, "If anyone asks, you're Jewish." I turned to Dad who just shrugged. We kept following.

Moises walked ahead and met a man at the door. They talked for a few minutes until Moises pointed to us standing down the block a bit. They waved us in. Inside Moises introduced us to the man he was talking to who was ran the center. It was a place for any Cuban Jew passing through Jamaica to get a little more help than what the Cuban Refugee Center was able to offer. Inside there were stacks of shirts, pants, underwear and, most importantly, socks. I think the man knew we weren't really Jewish, but he didn't seem to care. True generosity knows no bounds. He told us to grab a few of each. Joaquin and I ran up and down the rows overwhelmed. Dad had to remind us that we weren't in any positing to be picky. Grab something and be grateful.

No one was more grateful than Mom, who burst into tears when we came home with a bag full of new clothes. "God bless Moises and that organization," she said. It didn't seem appropriate at the time to call out the irony. Catholic woman asks God to bless the fine work of the Jewish Community. In a few days though that was good for a few laughs, even from Moises. We saw him many more times in Jamaica, and he and my father remain close to this day. When asked why he did what he did for us he had a very simple answer, "At times like this we have to be Cubans first. If not, we'll forget what it means. What it really means."

Our last weeks in Kingston passed without incident. Mom assembled a new sock ball, so Joaquin and I were content. We did take in a bit of culture on one occasion. We went downtown to watch Jamaicans celebrate the second anniversary of their independence from Great Britain. I had no idea Jamaica had been an independent country for only two years, but it did help explain the poverty. I had learned all about Cuba's history of European imperialism. If Jamaica's situation was only a fraction like Cuba's, then it had only been two years since Jamaica's leaders actually had Jamaica's best interest in mind. I was happy for the Jamaicans I saw jubilantly marching. The country had a long uphill climb ahead of them, but they had the first and most important ingredient: freedom.

Just a few weeks before we left, another exciting event took place. A taxi pulled up to the house one day with a young Cuban couple and their two little girls. They were staying in another room in the house, and no one was more excited than Mom. Although she tried and tried, Mom was just unable to communicate with Mrs. Creeks, and she was having gossip withdrawals. I don't think she had ever gone that long without talking to another woman about whatever it is they talk about. With this new family, Mom finally had a friend she could yap away with. The new family didn't change my life at all other than having to sit at a more crowded dinner table, but seeing others in the same situation as us was reassuring. We were just one family out of a whole fleet of families making the exodus. The Cuban identity, the true identity that Moises talked about, would have a chance to live on in America. I'm proud to say it still lives on today.

16

"We're only a few hours from freedom." Dad said those words on a daily basis in Jamaica. It was his answer to any complaint. I'm sick of being stuck in this house. If I have to eat *that* again I'm going to lose my mind. I've spent the last two months asleep on the floor! "It's OK. We're only a few hours from freedom."

The words, however well intentioned, brought little relief until September 4, 1964, which also happened to be Joaquin's birthday. On that day, the words took on a literal meaning. Before we left the house that morning, Mrs. Corrales, the young mother of the new Cuban family that moved in, presented Joaquin with a card wishing him a happy birthday and a great life in America. It prefaced another somber goodbye for Mom who had grown close to Mrs. Corrales and cared for her daughters as if they were her own. Saying goodbye to Mr. and Mrs. Creeks was no easier; the two of them had put up with so much during our time in Jamaica.

The two Creeks boys made a brief appearance to our send-off to wish us a bright future, but the words were forced by the powerful glare of Mrs. Creeks. Frankly I didn't mind. The only thing I would miss about them was the music they played. A few weeks before we left, Noah played a song called "I Want to Hold Your Hand" by "some English group" called The Beatles. To avoid giving him any satisfaction I told them that I didn't like the song, but that was a lie. I loved it the first time and would continue to love it the next seven hundred thousand times I would hear that song in America. That English group turned out to be a big deal, and like most kids in America, The Beatles grew into my favorite band in the late '60s and early '70s. Maybe Noah and Donavon weren't so bad after all.

As soon as we stepped out of the cab, Dad just couldn't help himself. "We're only a few hours of freedom," he said to a flurry of laughter from the rest of us. Everything went right that morning, no delays, nothing. We strapped in and took off. We were finally America bound. For thirty minutes we experienced nothing but jubilation – until a landmass appeared below the plane. This time we didn't have to ask what island that was. We knew the geography of that part of the world. We flew over Camaguey, Mom's home-town. The sight of Cuba brought tears back to her eyes. She didn't blink for twenty minutes while she gazed out the window. None of us said a word until she pointed at a cluster of lights to the north-west. "Is that light my sister's home in Ciego?"

It probably wasn't Ciego, just another town, but the words kicked me in the gut anyway. Raul and Carlos were still down there, along with my aunt, uncle and grandparents. One of those houses was the home where the "Kings" once reigned. Ciego would never be the same. We were moving a couple hundred miles an hour, but during those moments the plane hovered over Cuba too heavily weighed down by our sorrow to move. Fields and houses, forty thousand feet below us, appeared as clear as the pictures in the unopened magazines tucked under our seats. Then there we were riding our bicycles down an unpaved country road. Raul led the pack. Joaquin and I were behind him, racing for second; and Carlos manned the rear. What adventures lay ahead? I couldn't say. The road was long and twisted.

Next, only the Straits of Florida lay below us. Cuba was gone from my sight forever. The stillness of the sea was sobering. I knew I couldn't trust my eyes that told me that the blue went on forever. It would end and with it this journey when we reached the land on the other side. I don't know what was happening in Mom or Joa-quin's minds, but a quick glance down the row told me they were each caught up in their own private pondering.

Always on cue, Dad suggested it was time to celebrate Joaquin's birthday, this time just us as a family – well, us and the flight atten-dants. Originally his birthday cake was a batch of cookies that came with our on flight meal, but the attendants brought over a real slice of cake for Joaquin. They seemed just as excited as we were. After a few refusals by Dad (he didn't want to let our celebration disturb the entire plane), the attendants led us in the "Happy Birthday" song. It was my first experience with an English-speaking birthday celebration, and I did my best to hum along since I didn't really know the words. It wasn't my birthday, but to me the song was a welcome. Welcome to our country, our language – which you sound ridiculous trying to sing in at the moment, but fear not you'll catch on – our culture, our freedom, everything. We value you and we're glad you could join us.

Sure, some of that was a 12-year-old boy's wishful thinking. We weren't even over U.S. soil yet, but I was starting to feel American. The jubilation grew as the Florida coast sprang from the ocean, and then again when the pilot alerted us that we would be beginning our descent to land. The city of Miami, alive and buzzing, became the only thing in view. From up there, the boulevards looked like endless racetracks for toy cars and the skyscrapers looked like bea-cons of hope as the sun's rays reflected off their glass exteriors.

The near-botched landing we experienced in Mexico was still fresh on our minds, but our excitement eclipsed any traces of fear. The plane dove towards a sliver of concrete below that would serve as our landing strip. Mom closed her eyes during a prayer of protection; Dad sat beside her expressionless, likely contemplating the next stop rather than embracing the moment's triumph. One day I would learn that's the curse of a father, eyes always three hurdles ahead. The run-way was clear as day below us, then just a short drop below. I couldn't tell if it was a rough or soft landing. As soon as rubber made contact with asphalt I felt nothing but relief. We made it. We were free.

• • •

The Miami Airport shook with life. I watched plane after plane take off and land, first from the window of the plane, then from the terminal that provided a spectacular view of the buzzing airport. We moved at a crawl, but I didn't mind. There were so many sights to take in, excitement in every direction. We worked our way through the long lines of customs and showed an official our passports. He reviewed them, stamped them, gave us a not-quite forced smile and said, "Welcome to America."

Once again, we met another friend of Dad's at the airport. I was beginning to wonder how he knew so many people. No matter what city we landed in there was an old friend waiting to take us under his wing. It was a testament to the great work Dad did throughout his career. Mr. Oliva, Moises, so many people were willing to take up their time to help us. Our greeter in Miami was named Luis Telnes. You may remember Luis. He was the friend who took his wealth to Miami via expensive watches on the tiny arms and wrists of his nieces and nephews.

I remembered Luis well and picked him out of the crowd. He hurried over to us and offered us warm embraces. "Welcome to America," he said. I wouldn't get tired of hearing that anytime soon. He wasted no time showing us the beautiful sights of Miami and the marvels of American capitalism. We ate lunch at a restaurant where we could sit on a patio and look out across Miami Beach. Everywhere I looked there were pretty women with men following them around. It seemed like all people did in America was sit on the beach and enjoy the company of friends and family. Of course, in about an hour, I learned that wasn't true, but America was a place where no one was scared to enjoy himself.

After lunch we went for a stroll. Mom couldn't help herself. She stopped at every window and admired what was inside. Occasionally she would point out a designer that used to be available in Cuba or a dessert she ate at a Havana resort decades before. "Let's get it!" She repeated and repeated, and a few times Luis obliged her request. Dad looked ill watching Luis' unending generosity. I saw flashy cars, shiny jewels in store windows and synchronized streetlights.

Everything I saw that day convinced me that I was in a place more prosperous than I could fathom, but window-shopping could get me only so excited. What really did it for me was the air conditioning unit in our hotel room that first night. I'm sure one or two A/C units had made their way onto Castro's summer home or some fancy Havana resort where Russian delegates stayed, but I had never seen one with my own eyes. It was like something out of a Jules Verne novel. I turned it to medium before I went to bed and fell asleep over the buzzing it created after a few minutes.

At about two in the morning I woke up shivering. Dad was sitting in a chair with his feet propped up staring out the window. "It works too well," I said, but his mind was elsewhere. I took a few steps towards him and he shook his head like he was loosening cobwebs. I repeated my assessment of the A/C unit. He laughed and looked over at the buzzing machine. He hadn't noticed the chill in the room.

"Everything works here. Everything is possible here."

17

Most of what I thought I knew about the U.S. came from old movies and TV shows. I thought all Americans had light skin and blond hair like the actors we saw on TV. Definitely not true. I thought Americans had limitless supplies of beef. That's what I had heard from disgruntled Cubans when we waited in food lines. Americans had more food with more variety than I even knew existed, but it certainly was not limitless. For some reason, Mom believed that Americans all spoke softly unlike Cubans who had a tendency to scream and talk over each other. I don't know where Mom got that idea. It might have had a sliver of truth to it, but she thought way too much into it. "Speak softly," she told us when we visited public restaurants or stores. "Speaking loudly is a bad Cuban habit." I never got the impression that Americans cared how loudly I spoke, but we did what she said anyway.

There was one thing about America I was right about. During our last years in Cuba, gum – that's right chewing gum – became a hot commodity. It didn't come in our food rations and we didn't have spare money for unnecessary, albeit spectacular products, like chewing gum. I probably wouldn't have been able to find it if I tried, but there was another way for Cubans to get gum. Cubans who had migrated to America hid strips of gum within the folds of letters they sent to their relatives in Cuba. From time to time, neighborhood friends would come around boasting about the tiny piece of chewing gum they received. It took on a powerful meaning. Cuba is a place without commodities like gum, but America was teeming with gum. That was the perception anyway.

Well gum didn't grow on trees, but there was a lot of it. The very first thing I bought when we disembarked the plane was a pack of Bazooka Bubble Gum for a quarter. I chomped right through the pack as if the sticky substance provided lifesaving sustenance, or any sustenance for that matter, blowing bubbles and making obnoxious noises all the while. Of course, the noises mortified Mom, and she told me to throw it out. She understood that chewing gum was my way of enjoying American freedom, but, as she made very clear, that did not entitle me to be rude.

Something I painfully learned is that Americans really didn't know a thing about Cuba. Culturally, they confused us with Mexicans or lumped all people of Latin-American origins into one category. Cubans don't eat tacos; I don't know how many times I heard that one. The Americans I met seemed to fall into one of two categories. Some believed that Cuba was a miserably, poor country without any modern infrastructure. I remember people being surprised that we had a TV in our home or even a refrigerator. They thought Cuba was still stuck in the Colonial Age.

Other Americans had a wonderful perception of Cuba because they had been on vacation there in the decades before Castro. Cuba was a popular honeymoon spot in the '50s, and the Americans that chose to celebrate there were not disappointed. I recall a man I met in Miami going on and on about how beautiful the avenues of Havana were. He described catching a glimpse of the Havana skyline at dusk decades before from a ship with more details than I could have used. It made me sad. I would probably never see it again. Because Cuban honeymooners remained confined to the "touristy" spots of the island, they believed Cuba was wealthier than it really was. Few Americans knew the truth, which was somewhere in the middle.

The glimpses of American culture that made their way to Cuban came to a sudden halt in 1959 when the island was almost entirely shielded from American influence. I had a few years worth of music to catch up on in America, but thanks to Donovan and Noah, I had a head start. On one of our first nights in Miami we had dinner with Luis and his family. A niece of his, Desi, who was about my age, played a few tracks from "Meet the Beatles," the group's first album that was released in America. She went on and on about Paul McCartney's hair, voice, and teeth. Listening to her was unbelievably irritating, but I liked those songs as much as the one Noah played.

• • •

Planting our feet on American soil was the most important step on our journey, but we were not yet able to rest. We were still half a continent from reuniting with our relatives and settling in Wisconsin. After our slow churning two months in Jamaica, our week in Miami moved too quickly for any of us to take in as much as we wanted to. We spent a day at Opa-Locka Military Base outside of Miami for what Dad called a paperwork stop. I spent the whole day there sitting on a bench with Mom, Joaquin and Lidia while Dad filled out document after document and answered questions. The men at the base asked him a hundred questions about the military activity in Cuba, the locations of bases and troop movements. I doubt Dad was able to tell them anything worthwhile, or anything that they did not already know, but he did his best to help them. I wanted to tell them about my experience at the base in Ciego, but Dad told me not to. I don't think he really believed me in the first place, but he probably didn't think it was a good idea for a twelve year old to be put through a military interrogation.

We spent a few days at the Cuban Refugee Center in Miami, also called Freedom Tower. By the time we got there, the center had already been in operation for several years and aided thousands upon thousands of Cubans. Freedom Tower was where the children who left Cuba through *Operación Pedro Pan* were originally housed and cared for. The "Ellis Island of the South" was yet another source of help that I'll be forever thankful for.

I'll never forget driving down an avenue lined with palm trees, and seeing the tower rise twenty stories high topped with a dome cap. It resembled the oldest buildings in Havana in its colonial, grandiose style. All around the tower hung interchanging Cuban and American flags. What would happen to someone in Cuba if they flew an America flag? I didn't want to think about it. It was a testament to America's willingness to take on the exiled and make them their own. Seeing that tower probably gave me only a fraction of the sensation that millions of European immigrants felt when they first saw the Statue of Liberty from ship decks on route to Ellis Island, but it was a powerful moment nonetheless. Just like Lady Liberty a thousand miles north, the tower served as a welcome beacon and a symbol of why we embarked on our journey in the first place.

The Cuban Refugee Center gave us clothing and basic necessities like toothpaste. Each of us was given a physical, and volunteers ensured we had everything we needed to make it to Wisconsin. Thanks to our relatives, we were better off than most, but for many refugees the center was nothing short of a miracle. It provided care for the sick and fed the hungry. It helped Cubans find work and places to live. Just as importantly, the center kept records on every Cuban who had passed through. Many Cubans arrived without actually knowing where their relatives in the U.S. were. The Center helped to reunite those families.

During our last days in Miami, we took in the sights of the city and shopped, well window-shopped. We had a few dollars now, but most of what we saw was still beyond our reach. Yet, for some reason, it brought all of us joy to see clothes and electronics that were beyond our means and restaurants we couldn't quite eat in yet. They were trophies to aspire to. Maybe one day soon Dad could walk these streets and buy himself a fancy radio as a reward for his hard work. Here no one could take it away.

18

Days later we were on another plane, a smaller, older aircraft that felt significantly slower than the two mammoth jet aircrafts that took us to Jamaica and then to Miami. I scanned through the hundreds of pictures of planes that I had committed to memory and decided it was probably a DC-6 because of its four propeller engines.

We made short stops in Ft. Lauderdale and Cincinnati, then a long stop in Chicago's O'Hare Airport where I had the chance to put more of my plane knowledge to the test. Through large glass windows in the terminal, Joaquin and I watched plane after plane land and take off. I stared at them until the names came to me. I saw Boeing 707's, more DC-6's and its cousins the DC-3 and DC-8. Joaquin made it his mission to time how often planes took off. He swore it was one a minute. The rest of the family sat in the lobby alternating between impatient waiting and sleep, but Joaquin and I would not have been happier at a toy store. Chicago felt like the center of the world. I saw hundreds of planes from dozens of airlines flying thousands of people to destinations all over the world.

After a couple of hours of plane watching, we boarded an even smaller plane to carry us on the last, short leg of our journey. Finally, we were heading to Madison, Wisconsin, our new home.

As we took off, I caught a glimpse of a massive highway (I-90 I would later learn) and was astonished by the width of the road and the number of cars. I couldn't help but laugh when I thought of the *Santiago-Havana* that connected Cuba from end to end. That was the largest road in Cuba, yet the entire road could have fit into only one side of I-90 with room to spare.

An hour later, we began our descent to land. The landscape was endless, lush with several, breathtaking lakes that surrounded the city. The spectacular view was the first glimpse of my new home, another first on a trip full of firsts. Before stepping foot off the plane, I felt pride in my new city. If nothing else it was pretty.

The landing was uneventful. Gathering our belongings and calmly following the line off the plane was a test of will power. I wanted to leap out the window, land on the ground and kiss it. Outside we found Uncle Orlando and Aunt Vilma and all of their children frantically waving at us. After embracing Vilma, Mom had to sit down. We had endured a near botched plane landing, months of sleeping in one room, and having no choice but to rely on others' charity. Every burden she had carried for months rolled right off her shoulders. Dad didn't cry, but he embraced his brother, Orlando, forcefully and held him tight for a minute. He was excited to see him no doubt, but he was also more thankful than words could express to his brother who had funded a large part of our journey.

Outside of the airport, I took a breath. The breeze was cool on that September evening. It tasted different from the air in Cuba or Miami. It had no hint of the sea, but no hint of Castro either, a fair trade.

Our first night was easy, so much so that Mom told us not to get used to it. St. Dunstan's Church, a church from neighboring Middleton, Wisconsin, set us up in a motel room that was slightly above average by American standards, but to us it might as well have been a luxury suite. The TV worked and the mattresses were clouds to sink into. Best of all, we had two rooms. As much as I love my family I was sick of our slumber parties. When Mom opened up the refrigerator she gasped. "My God! Is anyone hungry for a steak?"

There were a lot of things we would have to worry about soon. We needed a permanent home, Dad needed to find work, and we also had one colossal language barrier to contend with. I remember English coming to me easily. I was young and my brain was still ripe for that kind of knowledge. But, for my parents, learning a new language would be a battle. Nevertheless, all of those troubles could wait. For the next few days we explored our new city and tried the local cuisine, McDonalds. The place was new to me, but my cousin recommended the hamburgers and french fries. I'll never forget what I paid for a cheeseburger, french fries – which in no way appeared French – and a drink: 72 cents.

Within days, our first major hurdle was solved thanks to the same church. A kindly man from the church came by one day to show us an apartment nearby. His appearance was what at the time I considered "All-American." He wore a suit with neatly combed hair, was clean-shaven, broad shouldered and, most notably, blond. He smiled when we tried to explain in broken English how grateful we were to him and his church. We loved America, we told him, now and forever.

He drove us a few miles to an apartment complex on Harvey Street that, although not extraordinary, had one major perk. Not even 100 yards from the entrance of the complex stood yet another McDonalds. How many of these places are there? He took us up a flight of stairs into a simple apartment fully equipped with furniture donated by other churchgoers. The apartment came stocked with an old black-and-white TV, an AM-FM radio, a living room couch that was big enough to fit all of us, and a bed for each of us. The place was modestly sized, but we'd experienced much worse. We didn't need a lot; we just needed a place that everyone could agree was ours.

It was not just since we left Cuba that we had been homeless. Even during our last few years in Cuba we didn't have a home we could truly enjoy, well my parents couldn't anyway. I just blissfully lived my life, but Mom and Dad spent day and night worrying about the future of our family in a home that did not belong to its inhabitants but to the "people." I remember how wonderful it felt that night to sleep in a bed that was mine. But despite how I felt, my emotions could not even put a dent into the relief my parents must have experienced that first night in our new home. Years worth of burdens were finally laid to rest.

• • •

We made a much-anticipated trip to our neighboring McDonalds the next day for lunch. It was close enough to sprint to, so Joaquin and I raced to the door, and then to the counter. We ordered the same 72-cent meal that we ordered a few days before. That part was easy. It was a value meal, so all we had to say was a number. But today we were also having a special treat.

"Meelk shake, pleez."

"Sure, what kind?"

"Chalk, um, chalk-uhhh –"

"Chocolate?" There it was. We nodded our heads like bobble-heads in an earthquake. "Coming right out."

We would come back so often that the cashier wouldn't even have to ask us what we wanted. Once my English improved, I made a point to say "chocolate" even though he already knew. In those days, nutrition and health were not the concern they are today, but I don't think that would have swayed us. It was cheap, close and delicious, for a recent Cuban exile to expect anything more was asking for too much.

I was nearly done with the shake before my parents were even done ordering. When my Mom sat down, she was appalled. "Don't you want to savor that? Your friends in Cuba don't have enough milk for one. *Recuerda la suerte que tienes.*" Remember how lucky you are. She was right. Yet again the deliciousness of a chocolate shake triggered feelings of guilt. I sat in silence for much of the meal watching a group of teenagers, local high school kids gathered for an after-school snack, tearing through burgers, inhaling milkshakes and goofing off. The smallest of the group slapped the biggest one with a hamburger bun triggering a short chase through the restaurant. They calmed down, ate some more, and took off in their fancy muscle cars, but they left half-eaten burgers and stacks of fries behind.

"How can they do that?" I asked Mom, pointing to the pile of "trash" on their table.

"They don't know better. They've never seen what it's like somewhere like Cuba."

I didn't think ill of the teens, but I vowed that years of American luxuries would not turn me into one of them. I didn't need to feel guilty every time I tasted a milkshake, but I couldn't forget that I was the lucky one. Milkshakes from then on carried a special significance for me, a symbol of what I had that others didn't. A reminder of the months when we were nomadic and of the struggles my parents endured.

19

A few days after we were moved into the apartment, we got a visit from Reverend Childs of St. Dunstan's Church. He came over to make sure we were settling in well. Once he was through with the basics (clothing, food, and shelter), he glanced over at us kids sitting impatiently in the corner.

"And how old are you three?" 12, 11, 8, we answered. "It's time you kids get back in school. Tomorrow I'll come by and pick you three up in the morning and take you to Hoyt Elementary. It's just down the road. What do you think?"

I just nodded. I knew this day was coming eventually, but I was terrified. I knew maybe twenty words of English. How could I make friends, how could I learn?

Mom was thrilled. Joaquin and I had spent the last two years either in a school my parents hated or out of school entirely, and Lidia had been only home schooled. It was time for a stable, non-invasive educational environment for the three of us. She spent that evening picking out the best of all of our inherited outfits. Dad caught us up on all the American history he remembered.

"Remember, Thomas Jefferson wrote the Declaration of Independence. Abe Lincoln freed the slaves. George Washington was the first president. Ben Franklin … uh, he … well let's see. You know what, just remember his name. What else? American rebelled from the British in 1776; they won World War I and II, and ... oh, yeah, the Civil War, 1860 something. That was Lincoln too."

Was that it? The entire history of America. I felt less sure of myself than I did before he shared his knowledge. I didn't sleep a minute that night.

Reverend Childs showed up just when he said he would. We hopped in his car and made the short drive to the school. He could sense our nervousness, and he did his best to appease us. "You'll be pros with English in no time. And don't worry about the kids. They'll be your friends soon too. Just you see."

Once there, he led us into the office and spoke with the principal for a few minutes. Then, she came out and welcomed us. She had the look of a woman who could be terrifying if you crossed her, but in that moment she radiated nothing but warmth. She said some words about Cuba and how happy she was that we could join her school and country. I felt a little better.

Then, I felt a lot better. The principal walked us through hallways full of posters and bulletin boards. We dropped Lidia and Joaquin off at their new classrooms, and then she led me to the 6th grade hall. Inside I met Miss Jones who instantly gave me a bear hug. I thought I had seen her from somewhere, but that was impossible. She took my hand and directed me to my desk, and then it came to me. She was Jackie Kennedy, or her sister, at least a cousin. Her dark hair shined with her smile, and her eyes sent rays of warmth across the room.

In words I could only half understand, she told the rest of the class my name and where I was from. I felt twenty sets of eyes on me, a real-live Cuban. Each student was instructed to go to the board and write his or her name, and then say it. I'll never forget that Eric Anderson went first. He hopped right out of his desk, scribbled his name and then spoke it with the bravado of a rock star. He strutted back to his desk, giving me a nod as he passed. Eric would become my first friend in America and later play first base on my little league team. I'll forever be grateful of his sincerity that day. He set the tone for the entire class and I truly felt welcome.

It wouldn't take me long to grow accustomed to my new school and class, thanks mostly to Miss Jones who served as a remarkable ambassador for America. Initially, the biggest shock was a mid-morning break that the class took to drink milk. At first I thought the break was for a special occasion, but the second day I was handed a carton of milk again, then the third day and every day after. After I was sure that it was something I could count on, I told Mom about the free milk.

"God bless these Americans. *Recuerda la suerte que tienes.*"

Her joy was short lived though. The mention of milk triggered memories of waiting in those food lines, taking what *they* gave you. Even good news could not appease the frustration and sadness that went with her wherever she went. Part of me regretted even bringing it up, I should have known better, but I couldn't help but reflect on how perfectly something like milk could sum up the differences between the two countries. In Cuba, milk is a protected luxury to be carefully allocated. In America, it's handed out to children daily.

• • •

With us kids in school, my parents could settle into a routine. The burden of rebuilding our lives fell most heavily on Dad who worked two jobs during those years. By day, he worked at the University of Wisconsin's library. He helped shelve books, especially in the Spanish section. By night, he worked as a bellboy at the Park Motor Inn across town. I was too young to appreciate what it meant back then for a man who spent most of his life rising through the ranks of the banking profession to have to work at two low-paying jobs just to provide for his family. Looking back on it now, I'm amazed with the patience he showed. His willingness to do whatever it took for us to have a better life is truly inspiring.

He did this for years. Work one shift, hop on a bus, work another shift deep into the night, and then take another bus home. He'd sleep a few hours then get up and repeat. On Friday and Saturday nights he worked even later at the hotel to earn as much in tips as he could. His most lucrative nights were Saturdays in the fall when the University of Wisconsin played their football games. He joked that he made his money from drunk people getting too upset or too excited about the games. Staying late though meant missing the last bus, and many times he was forced to walk home. I looked up the distance years later, once the Internet made it very easy to do things like that. It was almost five miles, seeing that figure made me sick. I always knew those years were grueling for him, but I never realized just how much he gave. I tried to stay up and wait on him with Mom once, but I woke up to his tapping me on the shoulder, telling me to go to bed. It was just a few hours shy of morning.

Mom found time to do little odd jobs in between cooking and caring for her family. Some days she cleaned houses while we were at school, other days she watched over the children of neighbors we came to know. Most of them were foreign couples who studied at the university with small children. This was hardly work to Mom who would quickly grow attached to any child she looked after and bring them into our family. One of these children, Arturo, practically became another brother for me. Arturo was the only son of a young Venezuelan couple that lived close by. He was a tiny, dark-haired, crying brat who grew into quite the Packers fan.

We all did. It was our duty as Wisconsinites. It didn't take long for us to get that message. Just a few weeks after our arrival, I sat down with Joaquin to watch our first Packers game – actually our first American football game with any team. It was a struggle to get our hand-me-down, 15-inch, black-and-white TV to show a picture. Kids today have no idea how lucky they have it when it comes to TVs. Maybe you've seen people banging on the side of a TV to try to get it to work. That and the antenna dance were a daily reality for us.

Getting the TV to work proved to be largely futile though. We couldn't make sense of the strange game on the television. All we knew was the team with a yellow helmet with a G on the side was the good team. I watched Bart Starr, the Packers' quarterback. If he cheered, I cheered. Before each play he'd point at defenders and yell commands to his teammates, even occasionally running over to one to speak into his ear. I had no idea what he was doing, but he sure looked cool doing it. Even to two complete football newbies, it was clear who was in charge. We watched the first inning and saw Bart throw a touchdown pass. Then the defense came out, created three pile-ups and ran off the field. The Detroit Lions – I learned the other team's name about this time – kicked the ball back to a Packer who stood by himself 40 yards behind his teammates as an entire mob chased him. Then Bart came back out, handed the ball to his friend who ran into three more pile-ups, and that was about the end of the first inning.

Then, I learned it was called a *quarter*, not an inning; and the kick was actually called a *punt*. There was some sort of significance to getting a *first down*, but I had yet to figure that out. It seemed a large part of the game was running head on into a crowd of people and pushing forward for a few inches. It was a lot of work for nothing. Why didn't they just let Bart throw the ball every time? That was a lot more effective. By the end of the first half the Packers had scored twice to match only one *field goal* from Detroit. The score was 14-3. I couldn't figure out why it was only worth one point when the Packers kicked the ball through those yellow poles, but it was three points when the Lions did it. The game was far too random for my taste.

Mid way through the second half, that rule and many others were clarified. This time around Detroit managed to score a touchdown, but that wasn't enough. By the time the clock ticked to 0:00, I was swollen with Packer pride and a football expert. The Packers were going to win it all that year, as long as they give up on that running nonsense and let Bart hurl the ball down the field every time. Whoever this Lombardi fellow was that ran the team clearly didn't know what he was doing.

The next day at school, I felt confident enough to join the kids playing football at recess. I didn't understand the formal method of picking teams, but I just stood with the offense regardless of which team it was. When someone said, "Hut!" I took off running, didn't get passed to, then ran back. By the end of the game they must have felt sorry for me because they offered me the chance to throw the ball. I was terrified, but I took it without hesitation.

I positioned myself a few feet behind the center and started pointing to various defenders. I had no idea what I was pointing out, but the first rule of football, as far as I was concerned, was do as

Bart does. It actually worked. A few defenders turned and gave each other confused glances, while others were overtaken by laughter as I yelled, "HAWWT!" The defenders tripped over themselves chasing my receivers down the field. I bobbled the snap, but recovered in time to scurry around the pocket and realize I was out of my league. No one wore a uniform and I could not remember whom I was even supposed to be throwing to. I figured the chubby kid chasing me was on the other team, so I ran away from him. Someone was ready to cut me off though, so I doubled back around the first clumsy pass rusher. I heard groans of "Throw the darn ball," so I did. I took a few strides forward and launched it at no one in particular using my whole body to create momentum like an outfielder heaving the ball into the infield. The spiral needed work, but the ball hung in the air and carried across the field. One of my teammates happened to be in the area and ran underneath it. He caught it and skipped completely by himself in the end zone.

I was barraged by high fives and lifted into the air by the biggest guy on my team. He carried me around in a circle as the rest of my teammates danced around us, mimicking my throwing motion. Across the field the other team screamed at each other, each player blaming another for their defensive lapse. The game was easy, I told myself. I'll be a Packer in no time.

The next day my luck caught up to me. The defense wasn't fooled by my pre-snap antics, and my wobbly throws fell into the wrong hands. I learned the difference between a forward pass and a fumble that day, and I also learned that there are few things worse than watching someone dance after returning your interception for a touchdown to win the game. I was broken for a minute until I caught my own teammates laughing at the dancer's best imitation of a rain dance. Maybe they didn't take this game that seriously after all. After a moment of feeling humiliated I laughed with them. By the third day, I learned that most kids were more concerned with what their next touchdown dance would be than actually winning. I decided I could relax too.

20

B y November it was colder than I knew was possible. We started wearing sweaters in September and could see our breath on October nights. I learned to dress in layers and not to talk or think about it. No one needed you to point it out; they already knew it was cold. I woke up one morning thinking that school was surely cancelled. How could they expect life to go on with this cold? But life did go on in Madison. Nothing short of a blizzard was enough to fluster the locals. But when I saw flurries of snow fall for the first time (in October!) I thought the world was ending.

Snow was one of many firsts for us during the fall of 1964: learning a new language, playing a new sport, attending a new school. I slipped on my first ice puddle and made my first set of American friends. Of all the firsts that I experienced though, few were as informative as my first taste of American politics during the presidential election that November.

We spoke a lot about it at school, and I even got called on a few times to try to relay to the class how the American system contrasted to the Cuban one. I struggled to articulate the words, but I think my classmates got the message. We had no choice. Castro was president. If that bothered you, well you better keep your mouth shut. I could see the shock in some of their eyes.

Miss Jones thanked me for telling my story then the class held a mock election. I was one of only a few students who voted for Senator Barry Goldwater. I didn't know that much about him, but Dad had told me about his strong stance against Castro and communism. That was enough for me. The real election went similar to our mock one. LBJ won in a "landslide." I learned a new word that day.

Goldwater was lost to history for the most part, but I never forgot that he was the first American politician who really spoke to me. He later wrote a book called *The Conscience of a Conservative* that I read in college. It was a very influential read in which he reiterated his belief in personal freedom and his hatred of communism. I saw him as a pioneer who took a pounding from his critics, yet his ideas remained. He may be one of the most influential losers of any election.

That election was significant for a number of reasons. Lyndon Johnson proclaimed during his campaign that he'd keep American troops out of Vietnam, yet a year later he began the massive escalation that would eventually send 500,000 soldiers there, a harsh lesson in trusting campaign rhetoric. Also, a lot of analysts thought the Republican Party would never win an election after that landslide. Yet they won seven of the next ten presidential elections.

• • •

By our first Thanksgiving I knew the name of almost every Packer and could recite most of their stats. I learned the four-down system and the difference between a tackle and a guard. I was done thinking I knew more than Lombardi although watching the team punt on every fourth down drove me off the wall. Joaquin and I played a lot of sandlot football games at a park across the street from our apartment. We now had friends to play with. I couldn't figure out what I liked more, throwing the ball or receiving it. I did know I hated playing defense though.

We tried to pass on our newly adopted culture to Mom as we watched the Thanksgiving Day games before dinner, but it was a slow process. "Did the Packers score?" No they're on defense. "When do they kick it?" It's called a punt. Dad was a faster learner, although when he actually had a chance to watch a game he was asleep in his chair by the end of the first drive. His workday was unforgiving.

We were truly able to appreciate the spirit of our first Thanksgiving. We celebrated the day with my aunt, uncle and cousins at their home. Aunt Vilma spent the entire day cooking the turkey while Mom helped her in the kitchen. Mom also brought a *flan* to give the festivities a unique Cuban flavor. It was fitting, a Cuban-American Thanksgiving. Before we ate, Uncle Orlando, who was a few years more experienced at being an American, related the story of the pilgrims and the first Thanksgiving with my cousins anxiously filling in the details. It sounded really familiar, men and women leave their homes searching for a better life, struggle, but persevere, then take a day to give thanks.

The meal was delicious and gave birth to my lifelong love of turkey. We laughed through most of it, but did give pause to say a prayer for Ignacio and everyone who was still struggling in Cuba. Mom pointed out that we had more food on our table than they would see in a month. Moments like this were nothing new for us. My parents were determined to never let us get lax in our appreciation of freedom. If they thought we had gone too long without reflecting, then we would hear a summary of the most recent letter Mom had received from Cuba. Or, she would remind us of those damn food lines. "*Recuerda la suerte que tienes.*"

We couldn't hang around long after our feast. Dad's relentless work schedule would resume the next morning, so we had to get home. We didn't live that far, but the holiday bus schedule turned our trip into a long one. As we sat in the empty bus, Dad told us how proud he was of us for how maturely we handled everything that had transpired that year. He told Joaquin and me that the mark of a man was being able to do what must be done for your family. He spoke of the meaning of the holiday and the adversity the pilgrims faced after a harsh winter. Our struggle was not over, but we were moving on towards better days. Be stronger for your struggles. The message sank deep.

• • •

Christmas wasn't a first. We'd celebrated the holiday our whole lives, but in a slightly different fashion. Cuba, like many Latin-American nations, followed the Catholic tradition of the Three Wise Men, or *Los Reyes Magos*, from the New Testament story. Kids wrote letters with requests of what they wanted for Christmas, but instead of addressing those letters to Santa they were addressed to the Three Wise Men. Around the holiday season shops decorated their stores with mannequins of the Three Wise Men and their camels, and the large department stores brought in the "real" Wise Men with live camels. It was just like taking your kids to see Santa Claus at a mall in America. Kids sat on their laps and told the *Magos* what they wanted for Christmas. The really exciting part was petting the camels.

December 25th held significance as the day of Jesus' birth, we'd go to Christmas mass and have a nice dinner, but the gifts were delivered on January 6th, The Day of Kings, by the Three Wise Men. That morning, kids would react no differently than they do in America on Christmas morning.

This tradition, however, was starting to die off around the time we left Cuba, and came to a complete end in the late '60s. Why the demise of a cherished holiday? Its religious undertones of course. It was still an official holiday until 1969 when Castro declared that it was interfering with the sugar harvest, but by then the holiday had lost its luster anyway. The Church was marginalized and any-thing associated with religion was discouraged. I'm sure Christmas celebrations continued in a lesser form, but the outward expres-sions of Christmas, trees and decorations, were largely diminished even by the time we left. The holiday made a resurgence in 1997 after Castro restored the official status of the holiday to celebrate Pope John Paul II's visit to the island – a plea for good publicity on Castro's part if you ask me.

Anyway, that was the past. We were now in America and wanted to adopt our new country's customs. Joaquin and I were too old for Santa, especially since we would have had to believe some ridiculous explanation for why the face of the holiday had just shifted from old men on camels to a jolly, fat man who rode a flying sleigh pulled by magical reindeers. But Lidia was still young enough to believe in such magic, and Mom was determined to let her be a little girl for another year at least. We told her that *Los Reyes Magos* couldn't make it all the way up to Wisconsin to bring her gifts, but Santa Claus could. We were in his jurisdiction now. After some explaining, she bought it. She changed the heading on her letter to "Dear Santa" and learned the names of all the reindeer.

Money was still too tight for us to go wild for the holiday, but one morning Mom called Joaquin and me to a meeting. Lidia was still asleep, so Mom quietly whispered her plea. Would we be willing to give up our gifts so that Lidia could experience the type of Christmas she deserved? I never got the sense that I had much of a choice, but I was perfectly willing to do it. The alternative was each of us getting a small gift. I'd rather my sister get something she really wanted. Joaquin agreed as well.

On Christmas morning, we awoke to one large gift under our tiny tree. Of course it was Lidia's, but at first she wasn't that excited. "Where are all the rest of them? Silvio and Joaquin's presents." She asked on the verge of tears. We hadn't planned for this, but Mom came up with an answer quick.

"Santa left their gifts at the wrong house. He'll bring them by in a few days when he gets a chance. He's really busy these days."

"Santa must need a better map or some better helpers. He's gonna get confused with all the kids in the world," Lidia said. We all laughed and she smiled. Now guilt-free, she unwrapped her present to reveal a Barbie set full of accessories. She shrieked with excitement when she saw it. I looked over at Mom who was on the verge of tears. She gave me a look that told me that she was proud of our sacrifice.

It felt good. I had certainly had better Christmases if you base it on the quality of my gifts, but never had I felt that I was truly embodying the spirit of Christmas like I did that morning. Watching her joy was worth a hundred gifts. After such a tough year, it was reassuring to know that she had not lost the blissful innocence that every 9-year-old girl should have. Laughter filled our apartment.

Joaquin and I spent the rest of the day outside playing football with the neighborhood boys. Playing in the elements was a rite of passage for growing Wisconsinites. It didn't matter if it was raining or snowing, we were going to play football on Christmas. We bundled up in layers and went out into weather that six months before would have crippled us. By the end of the day, we were drenched and covered in mud and snow, but it was all worth it.

That's the only time I can ever remember Mom not losing it when she saw us come home filthy. I guess that was our reward for giving our Christmas away to Lidia. It was a fair trade.

21

Winter turned into spring, and we turned more and more American. I sounded like an American when I spoke, and spring brought something that I certainly knew how to talk about: baseball. I befriended a kid named Jim, mostly because he was the only person in my class who liked talking about baseball as much as I did. Jim dreamed of playing in the Majors some day and idolized Tim McCarver, the great catcher for the Cardinals. With his help, I learned the names of every team and could name as many players as I ever could from the Cuban Winter Leagues. We played a game of catch one day after school, and after watching me throw a few times he offered me a tryout on his Little League team. I guess he was making sure I could do more than just talk.

I was more exciting than I had been about anything since landing in Wisconsin. The tryout took place on a beautiful March afternoon. I was expecting a formal practice session, but when I got there it was just Jim with a catcher's mitt. "Let's see that fastball you've been talking about."

I warmed up for a few minutes then took up his offer. I took my place on the mound as he crouched into a stance. He put down one finger, the universal symbol for fastball. I nodded as if that wasn't the only pitch I could throw. I went through my wind up and drove off the mound, hurling a pitch right into his glove. A perfect strike, so far, so good. I threw another, then another. Jim moved his glove all over the plate and each time I hit it. After twenty pitches Jim hopped up and ran to the mound.

"Where did you learn to throw like that? Are Cubans born to play baseball?" He gave me a high five, and, just like that, I was on the team.

A few days later we had a real practice. Jim's Dad, known simply as Coach B, immediately put me on the pitcher's mound. "Your job is to pitch," he said. I did not complain. I met the rest of the team and answered a hundred questions about Cuba. By the middle of the practice, I grew tired of their questions and wanted to have a little fun. In Cuba, we sleep in our cleats and wear our baseball uniforms to school, Joaquin's words coming out of my mouth. I had them going for a while.

I went home that day with a jersey in hand and an inflated ego. Mom detected my good mood as soon as I walked through the door. "I guess it went well?"

"Coach B said I'm the number one starter!" Her face lit up and she gave me a big hug before announcing the good news to the rest of the family.

"Just don't walk the first batter," she said. "He usually scores."

I didn't. The first game went as well as I could have hoped. My pitching was spotty at times, but we won. We won a lot of games that year, but more importantly, I guess, I made a lot of friends and was a part of something. Every time I took the mound or stepped into the batter's box I felt like I was representing Cuba, partly because my teammates would scream at me to show them my "Cuban Magic" or play "Cuban Baseball."

It started one day when I was playing right field. It was the second game in a few days and my arm was spent, so someone else was handling the pitching. Playing right field wasn't my favorite mostly because you were so far from the action. It was hard for me to stay focused. My mind would wonder as I stood out there kicking clumps of dirt below me.

A left handed batter was at the plate who had given us some trouble earlier with his hard hit balls to right, so I was playing deeper than normal. The at-bat dragged on with foul after foul, so my focus had all but evaporated. But then I heard a sharp ping that could only mean one thing: He hit the ball with the good part of the bat, and it was probably headed my way. Instinctively I took a step back. I had seen him hit two balls already over the right fielder's head, but this time it wasn't hit quite as hard. I pushed off my back foot and sprinted to shallow right. It was going to be close, so I lunged forward holding my glove out in front of me. I landed on my chest with a thud and a roll.

My gloved missed the ball, but my wrist didn't. Somehow the ball just stuck right where it landed and I pulled it in. It hurt, but I didn't tell anyone. I gave no indication that I didn't catch the ball normally. But I didn't fool anyone. When I got back to the dugout I was greeted by a host of laughter. My teammates tried to mimic my lucky catch. From that moment the belief was born that my Cuban blood made me lucky on the baseball field. "I'm so glad the Cuban is on our team." I embraced it. It was better than being called Ricky Ricardo.

I need to give out one last thank you. One day after a game, Coach B reminded the team that we all owed some money for our jerseys. He asked that we bring the money next game. My heart sank, that was it for me. My parents had bigger problems than paying for my jersey. They were so busy back then that they were hardly ever able to come to games, but I would tell them every detail about the game when I got home. I didn't even want to ask them for the money. That would only put extra pressure on them.

A few days later at practice, I walked over to Jim's Mom, Mrs. B, who handled all the uniform orders. I held my jersey as I stumbled with the words, "I ca-, can't play anymore." Instantly she got my meaning. She smiled brightly and told me not to worry about it. She'd take care of it. "You just pitch."

I leapt with excitement and gave her a hug and a hundred thank you's. So here it is. Thank you Mrs. B, and to everyone else who helped to give me that first Little League season. Your generosity helped ease my transition into America more than I can express. I was a part of something because of you.

I'm repeating myself, but I don't care. I was able to live the life I lived because of other peoples' generosity. Leaving Cuba, settling in Wisconsin, feeling like I belonged, none of these things could have happened without the goodwill of others. Americans aren't perfect, no one is, but nothing infuriates me more than when I hear someone say that Americans aren't charitable. They are, and I'm living proof.

• • •

By that summer I was a full-fledged American kid. I played two sports, I collected records, and I watched the Ed Sullivan Show a lot. I stayed up late listening to "Top 40" hits on the radio and mimicking the DJ's introduction. With so much music going digital these days, being a DJ (or "DJing") is a lost art. Actually, I tried to ask my son about it and he didn't even know what I meant. "DJing" meant something very different to him. He said something about electronic music or dub-step, whatever that is.

Back then the Disk Jockey would introduce the songs with as much creativity as the songs themselves. "Up next 'This Boy' by the FAAAAB FOOOOUUR." Once I got the records myself I would do my best interpretation of Don Sherwood, the greatest DJ of that time, to the puzzlement of Mom. She would come in and ask what on earth I was doing. It would probably sound even more ridiculous today to the iPod generation.

I was watching when The Beatles made their appearance on Ed Sullivan and I was hooked. I remember buying my first six records with Joaquin one day. "Nowhere Man" by The Beatles, "19th Nervous Breakdown" by The Rolling Stones, "You Are She" by Chad & Jeremy, "Eight Miles High" by The Byrds, "Over and Over" by The Dick Clark Five, and "These Boots Are Made for Walkin'" by Nancy Sinatra. My music tastes had long since left Cuba.

Joaquin and I figured out that being caught up on the pop music scene was essential to making friends and meeting girls in those days. The more music I discovered, the more Cuba seemed like a distant memory. Of course, my mother was always quick to remind me to "*recuerda la suerte que tienes,*" but, despite every pledge I made to maintain perspective, the truth is I was too absorbed in my new life to really remember my good fortune. Sometimes, though, God sent something or someone my way that made it impossible to forget my roots in Cuba.

One of my most vivid memories of Cuba was a day when I was ten years old and I ran right through a glass wall at a hotel near our home with my family. The hotel had a pool that was open to the public, and the pool was a frequent Saturday getaway for us. As we walked through the hotel, I saw a friend outside who I knew from school. For some reason it was imperative that I sprint outside and immediately say, "Hi." I had been to that hotel several times and I knew where the door was, but at that moment I had a mental lapse. I took a few strides, and then crashed right through the glass wall and landed in a pile of shards and blood. A hotel employee scooped me up and put me into a taxi. Mom was screaming at his heels and somehow still holding on to my brother and sister. I came out with only minor cuts, one of which left a scar on my arm that I have to this day.

As far as I was concerned, that took place in another world and in another life. But one day in Madison, while I was out to eat with my family, I heard a man behind me yell in Spanish, "Are you the kid who ran through a glass wall that morning in Havana?"

What? Who could possibly know that? I turned to find a Latin man pointing at me and laughing hysterically as he described to the men he was sitting with how I vaulted through a glass wall. "You'd be a millionaire if that happened to you in the United States," he said to Dad. Mom recognized him as the taxi driver from that day and we all shared a laugh. I was astonished. That was years ago and 1,400 miles away. What are the odds of being in the same restaurant as that man in Madison, Wisconsin, five or so years later?

22

As the months and years passed in Wisconsin, my siblings and I made a near complete adjustment. We were young and malleable, but my parents had lived a whole lifetime in Cuba. They didn't have the joys of Little League or the next Beatles album to enthuse them. For them, life in Madison was a constant struggle. While I was up late listening to records, Dad was up late working. I woke up early on Saturday mornings to get to baseball practice. Mom woke up early to watch Arturo after his parents dropped him off so that they could have an all-day study session. Making new friends was easy for us, the language came quickly and school provided a perfect platform to adapt to the culture, but my parent's friends were a couple thousand miles away.

Dad worked and worked, rarely letting his foot off the gas. But through his hard work, our lives slowly improved. Nearly everything in our apartment originally was donated. We were grateful, of course, but eager to upgrade at the same time. That took a back seat for about a year, but eventually Dad secured a firmer footing. It started in the kitchen (new plates, new forks) and then in the living room with a new lounge chair. Our old, ragged TV remained though. As immigrants, my parents had no credit in America.

Everything they bought was in cash, so large upgrades were really difficult. Finally, Dad had enough of that old TV. He spent the first few hours of one of his rare and precious days off trying to get the thing to show a picture, but he was unsuccessful. He walked out in a fury muttering about something called layaway.

A few hours later, he returned with a brand-new, 19-inch, full-color TV. The upgrade wasn't so much in the size, but in the quality. The colors were sharper and we wouldn't have to do the antenna dance every time we sat down to watch TV. Ecstatic, I helped him set it up and then sat down with him to watch a football game. By the end of the first quarter, he was snoring in his lounge chair. He spent too much energy buying it. I asked later that day how he bought it. I knew there was no way he had enough cash to buy it upfront.

He told me the story, and, to no one's surprise, he tied in a moral. He was standing outside the store window-shopping when he saw the perfect model, but it was well beyond his price range. He entered the store to ask a salesman if he could work out a layaway plan. He could pay it off over a month or two then take it home. The salesman seemed puzzled though. "Why not just buy the TV on credit?"

"I'm a Cuban immigrant," he said, "I have no credit." The salesman brought the storeowner, and he and Dad had a long conversation. As Dad told it, he practically told this man his life story.

"Forget layaway," the owner said. "You have an honest face. Put down what you can today then come by every two weeks and make payments." Dad took the offer and brought it right home. He said it was just like when he was a banker.

"Integrity and honesty are still the two most important items on a credit application. It's just a piece of paper. A rich man without integrity is no surer investment than an honest, poor man."

He went on to describe some of the farmers and small businessmen he loaned money to years ago in Cuba. If he went by the book he would have ran most of those men right out of his office, but he took a chance on his ability to judge character. He must have been good at it because many of them became his best clients. Some of them even grew into his good friends, like Luis who took us under his wing in Miami. This time he was on the other side of the desk, but he practiced what he preached. The TV was paid off early.

The TV was our first major purchase in the U.S. Sure, it was just a TV, but it meant a lot to Dad. It was a sign of a better future in America. I've met other immigrants over the years who place sentimental value on their first purchases in a new country. It's a sign of acceptance. My parents still have cheap Christmas ornaments that we bought during that first year in Wisconsin. There's nothing spectacular about them, but Mom would never replace them.

For Dad, that TV also had another meaning. He once took a chance on clients as a banker, and now someone did the same for him. I don't think he would have admitted it, but I could tell he missed his old profession. If anyone asked him what he did, he would say, "Well in Cuba I was a bank manager, but now ...." What he did for a living then was out of desperation. Banking was his trade, his passion and source of pride. Maybe deep in his ambitions he dreamt of doing it again, but that was nearly impossible in America. Who would hire an immigrant who spoke little English for such a prestigious position? Life can surprise you though.

For three-and-a-half years, he grinded through two jobs and a 16-hour or more workday. Early in 1968, at his hotel job, he struck up a conversation with a guest as he held the door for him. Part of his job was describing some of the hotel's services, pointing out the pool or the bar for example. This particular guest noticed Dad's accent and asked him where he was from.

"Cuba."

"That's what I thought. I have a Cuban friend in Milwaukee, Mariano Benet."

I wasn't there, but Dad told this story enough times that I might as well have been. Dad stopped dead in his tracks when he heard the name.

"Benet?"

"What you know him?" He more than knew him. That was the president of the bank that Dad worked for in Havana, the man who once gave me a baseball card. The hotel guest gave Dad

Mr. Benet's number. "Give him a call, he runs the International Division of First Wisconsin Bank in Milwaukee."

Dad thanked the man, and immediately left his post at the door. He made the call, but got a secretary. Within a few hours, he got a call back; within a few days, he was a banker once again at First Wisconsin Bank. The pay raise was more than modest.

I'll never forget the day we came home and Mom told us the news. She was in tears. Our lives, my parent's lives in particular, were about to get a lot better. Dad would have a reasonable work-day. He'd be around on weekends. And he could do what he loved. He got lucky. He'd be the first to admit that. But the luck would have meant nothing had he not built his reputation over a lifetime.

We stayed in Madison until the end of the school year, and then followed Dad across the state. I was sad to leave Madison, the town that took me in; but, if anyone deserved a break, it was Dad. I left behind my Little League team and a handful of friends, but I knew that Milwaukee was the next step on our American journey – a journey that has never stopped improving.

• • •

After a few years in Milwaukee, I was more American than I was Cuban. I was a typical high schooler. I worked part-time jobs to earn money to take girls out on the weekends with my newly earned license. I increased my record collection and tried out for my school's baseball team. Cuba seemed an ever-more distant memory, but a history lesson brought me back to the island of my birth.

My 11th grade history teacher told us to open our textbook to a chapter on the Civil War. I flipped through the pages until I found myself staring at Abraham Lincoln's Gettysburg Address. I returned to a moment a decade earlier when my Uncle Joaquin recited the words of the speech that he so passionately believed in. At the time, it was a speech in a strange language about another country's belief in freedom. Now I was fluent in that language, and that country was my own. More importantly, that country's freedom was now woven into every fabric of my life. I read the words and felt goose bumps crawl up my arm. The speech was written to commemorate one of the most tragic events in American history, but Lincoln's passion transcends across centuries as a reminder that freedom must be cherished and is forever worth pursuing. That was the lesson Uncle Joaquin tried to pass on to me years before. That was the lesson that Cuba didn't learn until it was too late.

For those of us who no longer have to fight to pursue freedom, it is easy to forget how precious it is. Just as in Lincoln's day, the flame of freedom struggles to burn brighter. Every generation builds upon that fire, so that it may shine over every corner of the globe. With our diligence we can all ensure that the fire continues to light the path for future Americans and for those around the world who see its distant light as a beacon of hope. It shined so bright in my youth that my parents brought me here so that I may bask in its light, and it is now in the hands of a new generation to fuel that flame and ensure *that government of the people, by the people, for the people shall not perish from the earth.*